D0530401

From page to performance
A study book for drama

Don Shiach

CAMBRIDGE
UNIVERSITY PRESS

The author would like to thank Andy Piasecki, Lecturer in Drama and
Theatre Studies at Royal Holloway and Bedford New College, for his
valuable help and advice.

PUBLISHED BY THE PRESS SYNDICATE OF THE UNIVERSITY OF CAMBRIDGE
The Pitt Building, Trumpington Street, Cambridge, United Kingdom

CAMBRIDGE UNIVERSITY PRESS
The Edinburgh Building, Cambridge CB2 2RU, UK   http://www.cup.cam.ac.uk
40 West 20th Street, New York, NY 10011–4211, USA   http://www.cup.org
10 Stamford Road, Oakleigh, Melbourne 3166, Australia

© Cambridge University Press 1987

First published 1987
Eighth printing 1999

Printed in the United Kingdom at the University Press, Cambridge

A catalogue record for this book is available from the British Library

ISBN 0 521 33735 6 paperback

Front cover illustration:
**Gaudete; adaptation from the poem by Ted Hughes at the Almeida,
November 1986. Photograph by Donald Cooper.**

Contents

Contents

1 What is a play?

1.1 A play is a play is a play is a . . .

When we are reading a play script, we should always see the text as the springboard for performance. Novels, and poetry for the most part, exist for the printed page. When we read a play text, we are reading the words that characters are due to speak on a stage; we read the stage directions that tell us what actors are to enact on a stage in front of an audience. This 'text' must be performed before we can say, 'This is a play'.

Looking at plays

Drama is a performing art. Drama is not a branch of literature. The essence of drama is live performance in front of an audience. Theatre has an immediacy, a 'here-and-now' impact that can create a unique bond between performers and audience, a shared experience which, at its very best, is utterly compelling and absorbing.

Playwrights write plays for audiences who have assembled in a public place to watch a theatrical performance. The 'audience' for novelists are individuals sitting by themselves reading words printed on pages. 'Live' audiences affect the way actors interpret the dramatist's words and actions on stage. This has to be emphasised because plays are often analysed in the same way as novels and short stories are, as though the text written on the page is the play. Thus, characters are analysed, motivations explained, themes explored in almost exactly the same way as these aspects of novels are discussed.

But the language, theatrical conventions and techniques playwrights use are clearly not the same as are used by novelists. The craft of writing for the stage is quite distinct from the novelist's art (although many novelists have tried writing for the stage with very varying success). The theatre has a language of its own – a theatrical language. Theatrical language refers to the specifically theatrical techniques that the theatre does not share with literature e.g. mime, movement, dance, costume and special effects.

What this book is about

A play, then, is only truly a play when it is being performed. However, that is not to say that plays are not worth studying as text, but that text must always be seen as a 'manual' for performance.

In this book we will be looking at how drama text can be 'translated' into performance. Most of our emphasis will be on how directors and actors can work on the text provided by the dramatist to turn it into a successful performance. We will be looking at extracts from plays of different periods and different genres and at various kinds of dramatic language. We will also be examining how dramatists use the opening scene of a play and how audiences are 'manipulated' in the theatre.

Questionnaire

To help to focus on some of the issues to be discussed in the first chapter, and to identify some of your own attitudes towards the theatre, look at the following questionnaire and then compare your answers with the responses of other people in your group.

1 Theatre has a more immediate and direct effect on the audience than cinema or television.
    i) agree   ii) disagree
2 Watching a play being performed live in the theatre is a completely different experience from watching on television.
    i) agree   ii) disagree
3 Reading a play is as valuable an experience as watching a play being performed.
    i) agree   ii) disagree
4 A theatre is always a purpose-built building where performers can put on productions.
    i) agree   ii) disagree
5 Theatre appeals to only a minority of the population.
    i) agree   ii) disagree
6 Theatre will always appeal only to a minority of the population.
    i) agree   ii) disagree
7 The formal aspects of an evening at the theatre are off-putting.
    i) agree   ii) disagree
8 The community, both at local and national levels, should subsidise theatre companies.
    i) agree   ii) disagree
9 'Alternative' or 'fringe' theatre that appeals to younger audiences cannot be described as 'serious' or 'real' theatre.
    i) agree   ii) disagree

1.2   What is a theatre?

The first purpose-built theatre in Britain was not erected until the mid-sixteenth century. Before then, dramatic performances of one kind or another took place in churches and church grounds, market squares, fairs and, indeed, any space that could be turned into a performing area.

Plays performed in the environs of churches, the 'Mystery cycles' (or 'Miracle plays') – plays about the lives of the saints and the New Testament – were popular in England from the thirteenth to the late sixteenth century. Trade guilds took the responsibility for mounting these performances, very often on wagons or platforms which could be moved from venue to venue. These Mystery plays are still performed today; several cycles of Mystery plays associated with particular places (e.g. York, Chester) have survived in script form.

Gradually, travelling professional players took over from the guilds. These actors would erect a platform in the yard of an inn, for example, and perform for audiences standing below.

1745.—Performance of a Dramatic Mystery at Coventry.

Mystery play: a nineteenth century print of a performance at Coventry in the middle ages. Note the raised, open-sided platform around which the spectators are congregated.

In 1576 a purpose-built theatre was opened in London. It was made
of wood, circular in shape and had no roof. The stage thrust out from
one wall into the middle of the yard, so that the audience surrounded
it on three sides. The wealthier members of the audience would
watch the performance from galleries above, and the less well-off
spectators would stand in the yard and look up at the performers.

William Shakespeare and contemporary playwrights such as Ben
Jonson and Christopher Marlowe, wrote plays for performance in
theatres like this, and for large audiences comprising a cross-section
of Elizabethan and Jacobean society. The type of stage and the kind of
audience they were writing for undoubtedly affected the plays they
wrote. Another important practical element they had to contend with
was the need to supply the companies of actors with roles that suited
their talents and numbers (remembering that in those times there
were no actresses; all female parts were played by males).

The Puritans under Cromwell closed the theatres in the 1650s,
because they were 'corrupting', but the reign of Charles II saw their
re-opening. Now they were built with roofs; they also became smaller
in size, which almost certainly meant theatre became the preserve of
the better-off in society. The other important development was the
move towards establishing the 'proscenium arch' stage. The proscenium arch is an arch or opening (frequently with curtains that can be
opened or closed on cue), with a permanent stage behind, which
effectively separates the audience from the performers.

The proscenium arch reigned supreme in theatres right through the
nineteenth century up to the present day. In Victorian times theatres
were built to house very large audiences again. There was no sense of
intimacy so that the theatre was largely given over to spectacle,
pantomime and melodrama. Gradually, however, the grip of the
proscenium arch has been loosened and numerous modern theatres
employ thrust stages (page 6), arena staging (where the audience
surrounds the performers and looks down on the action from above),
and theatre-in-the-round (page 6), where there are no intervening
arches or curtains between the audience and the performing area.

An Elizabethan playhouse (opposite): this drawing was done in 1965, but recent
research suggests that the gallery provided more divisions between spectators,
and less leg-room.

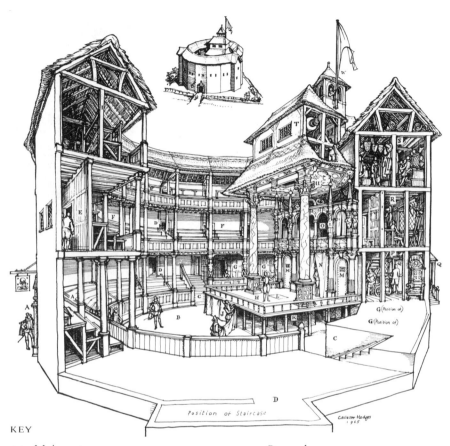

KEY

Open staging: the first major open stage theatre in Britain was constructed for the Chichester Festival Theatre in 1962. The audience sits at the front and sides of the stage.

Theatre-in-the-round: the stage at the Royal Exchange Theatre, Manchester opened in 1976; the audience surrounds the stage on all sides so that the actors have to 'act' to all sides of the theatre.

Just as importantly, there has been a movement away from the idea that drama performances can only take place in purpose-built theatres. After all, practically any space could be a performing area. Thus, performances may take place in pubs, community halls, schools, factories and in the open air (as in street theatre).

Some of those professionally involved in the theatre have been worried that it appeals to a narrow, largely middle-class section of the population, so they have decided to take theatre to the people, into their communities, rather than sitting back and expecting people to come to them. In a sense, then, this kind of 'alternative' theatre is going back to the roots of drama, to where it all began in Britain over a thousand years ago – in the community, in places where people congregate for purposes other than viewing theatrical performances. Part of this alternative theatre movement is the wish to encourage people to participate as performers. It is important to stress that theatre is a participatory art: you do not need to be a member of an audience all the time; you can choose to be one of the performers. There is no exclusive magic circle to which only the really talented can belong. Everyone can take part in drama.

An example of participatory street theatre from the theatre group 'Action Space Mobile': *Firestorm*, a spectacular in Manchester with 200 participants, based on Brecht's city poems.

The audience in a theatre

The audiences for Shakespeare's plays comprised a fair cross-section of the London populace of the time. One criticism of contemporary theatre is that audiences are largely split between those who will book tickets for light theatre: large-scale musicals (e.g. *Cats*), spectaculars (e.g. *Starlight Express*), popular thrillers (Agatha Christie's *The Mousetrap* has been running in one London theatre for over thirty years) and light comedies and farces; and on the other hand those drawn to 'serious' drama (e.g. productions of plays by Shakespeare or Chekhov, or modern dramatists such as Arthur Miller and Harold Pinter), the type of play the National Theatre, the Royal Shakespeare Theatre and other subsidised companies produce. This schism is sometimes categorised as the gap between the commercial and the subsidised theatre. Like all simplifications, this analysis is too sweeping, because the commercial theatre does mount productions of serious plays; and hugely popular successes often stem from the subsidised theatre. But despite this, the idea persists that serious theatre appeals to a minority audience and that too many practitioners in the theatre are not interested in reaching wider audiences.

Subsidised, commercial and alternative theatre

Some of the terms used above need to be defined. *Subsidised theatre* is theatre that receives financial aid from government or local councils. There has been a tremendous growth in the number of subsidised theatres in Britain during the last thirty years. Municipal theatres receive financial help in the form of grants from local councils (paid for by local rates). The government also provides grants to many theatres and touring drama companies through a body called the Arts Council, set up in 1946. Theatrical companies like the National Theatre Company on the South Bank in London and the Royal Shakespeare Company at Stratford and the Barbican, receive a large proportion of the sum allotted by the Arts Council for drama. The fact that subsidies are given in this way from local rates and government revenue is a recognition of the importance of professional theatre in the nation's cultural life. It also recognises the fact that serious and experimental theatre cannot usually survive without financial aid from the community. There are people, however, who argue that no financial aid should be given to theatre, or indeed any of the arts. They believe theatre should survive commercially and without aid. If enough people want to spend money on buying tickets for theatrical performances, then theatre will pay its own way. Another argument used by critics of grants to theatres is that the money is largely used to perpetuate a tradition of drama that appeals only to a small section of the population, so they question why the community as a whole should pay for it.

Commercial theatre usually receives no grants from any arts organisation or elected body. Theatrical companies finance productions on their own initiative and either stage them in theatres they themselves own, or hire theatres owned by other people for the duration of the 'run'. Most of the theatres in London's West End are commercial. The pressure on commercial managements and producers is to make money for the investors in a production. For a large West End musical, the initial production costs can run into millions of pounds. Even smaller productions hoping for a long run in a West End commercial theatre require considerable 'risk' capital (i.e. the money invested by the backers may well be lost if the show fails and is taken off after a short run). Therefore, the tendency is for commercial managements to cut down on risky ventures – a new play by an unknown dramatist, for example – and to go for what has been successful in the past – 'formula' plays such as thrillers, farces, comedies with famous stars from television, musicals and uncontroversial melodramas. The supporters of subsidised theatre claim that this timidity on the part of the commercial theatre is another argument for the importance of subsidised theatres because only they can risk putting on new plays or experimental work which may lose money at the box-office.

'Alternative' or *'fringe' theatre* is experimental, non-establishment theatre. Plays that explore new territory in terms of theatrical language, communication or theme very often surface on the alternative, or fringe, circuit. The term 'fringe theatre' originated from the Edinburgh Festival where an alternative festival consisting mainly of theatrical productions grew round the 'fringe' of the official Festival programme. Venues often include rooms in pubs, converted halls or churches, and community arts centres. This alternative theatre is intended to appeal to a younger audience than the average audience at a production in the subsidised or commercial theatre, and to those who are interested in a kind of theatre that breaks free from conventional theatrical styles. There are many critics of this alternative theatre who claim that it is second-rate, self-indulgent, obscure and lacking in high professional standards. Its supporters would claim that alternative theatre is the lifeblood of theatre, feeding in new ideas and talents to mainstream theatre. Tom Stoppard's play *Rosencrantz and Guildenstern are Dead* (1967), for example, first attracted attention in an Edinburgh Festival fringe production.

Fringe theatre: a scene from Steven Berkoff's *Metamorphosis* (adapted from Kafka) produced at the Mermaid Theatre, London in 1986, after starting life in a fringe theatre.

Going to the theatre

A 'night out at the theatre' involves more than just being part of an audience watching a play, or some other kind of theatrical entertainment. Going to the theatre involves other matters that affect how you react to the performance you witness – matters such as how formal or informal the occasion is, your feelings about the rest of the audience, the physical surroundings in which you watch the performance, whether you had to book your tickets in advance, the way the evening in the theatre is structured (e.g. intervals, separate acts), and the conventions of theatre (e.g. curtain calls at the end of a performance).

1.3   Drama: the co-operative art?

This book will primarily deal with how actors (meaning both men and women) and directors can turn text into performance. But it should be stressed that there are numerous other specialist practitioners involved in professional drama productions such as stage managers, set and costume designers, lighting and make-up experts and carpenters. Modern purpose-built theatres such as the National Theatre or the Barbican in London possess very complex technology. At the flick of a switch or the press of a button, stages can revolve and scenery can descend from the 'flies' (the space above the acting area from which scenery can be lowered when required for scene changes, and where scenery can be hung when not in use) or glide on from the wings. Film or slides can be projected on to a screen, a newscaster can inform the audience of important background information, and special lighting, audio or musical effects can be produced. This technological armoury is a far cry from the bare stages and simple props used by actors in Shakespeare's time, and some people complain that modern theatre is at times in danger of being swamped by technological wizardry.

However, the number of specialists that contemporary theatre requires does emphasise the fact that theatre is a co-operative art. Actors may receive most attention from the theatre-going public and the media, but actors are dependent on the plays dramatists write, on directors to guide them and all the other experts who stay in the background.

Actors and directors

The function of an actor in a performance of a play is to interpret his or her role within the context of the drama, to respond to the other actors on stage and to the audience, to be as faithful as possible to the intentions of the playwright and to perform his or her part in the manner that has been worked out during rehearsals with the director.

The director is generally accepted as being the person in overall charge of a production. The director usually chooses the cast, and advises the actors during rehearsals. The specialists (e.g. lighting and costume experts) have to discuss their contribution to the production with the director who tries to integrate these diverse elements into a coherent style and approach. A director usually has an overall interpretation of a play in mind – themes he or she wishes to bring out, aspects of character motivation that need to be stressed, a prevailing style that will shape the production.

A directors' theatre?

However, these definitions of the roles of actors and directors in the theatre, and their relationship to one another, are not universally accepted. The power of the director has grown considerably over the last fifty years so that it is now possible to talk about a 'directors' theatre', meaning that directors have become the most important creative influence in some theatre, more important even than dramatists (see 1.6).

Because this book is mainly about how actors and directors can best turn text into performance, it is perhaps worth pursuing the debate about the relative importance of the three roles – actor, director and playwright. Simon Callow, a contemporary actor, has strongly-held views about the roles of actors and directors in relation to the plays written for them by dramatists. In this extract from his book *'Being an Actor'*, Callow argues that the play and the playwright are best served by the actors taking more control, and the director playing a much less prominent part than has been the fashion in recent years.

> Starting at the end of last century and increasingly during the course of our own the theatre has become colonised by a determined group, the directors. It is they who run the theatres, they who determine policy, they who engage the artists who actually execute the work, and they who put the stamp of their personality on the production itself – the end product of all our labours. There are a number of consequences of this unchallenged hegemony which devolve most strikingly on the actors and the writers. Actors, quite clearly, have been stripped of initiative and responsibility. Writers, on the other hand, have been made to believe that the closest collaboration with a director is the only way in which the work will be properly realised. The director has interposed himself between actor and writer, claiming that they cannot speak each other's language. The assertion of the supremacy of the *text* has provided a stick with which to beat actors.
>
> *Acting* has become a pejorative term, used to delineate something impure, a product of the actor's egomania. The crucial element in the act of theatre, the actor's delight in the opportunities afforded him by the writer, has been abolished – outlawed by a breed of director who have little experience and no comprehension of the rich and vital processes of acting.
>
> The idea of a director's style, or indeed a company's style, seems inherently to threaten the individuality of the work itself. It is also easier and less interesting to impose such a style than to undertake the enormous task of entering the mind and hearts of people of another time – and as far as plays are concerned, any time before yesterday is another time.
>
> The important thing is to restore to each other the writer and the actor, without the self-elected intervention of the director claiming a unique position, interpreting the one to the other. We do not need an interpeter. We speak the same language, or at least we used to.

Comment and activites

▷   According to Callow, what control do directors nowadays usually have over productions?
      What effect does Callow believe this control has on i) actors; ii) writers?
      What do you think is meant by the phrase 'the supremacy of the text'?
      What does Callow identify as 'the crucial element in the act of theatre'?
      According to Callow, how is a play threatened by a director's or company's style?
      What is the solution put forward by Callow in the last paragraph of the extract?

▷   What is your own response to the arguments put forward by Callow in the extract?

▷   Improvise a scene in which a group of actors are rehearsing a scene with a very dictatorial director in charge. Choose a section from an actual play to rehearse and show the conflict that can arise when a director tries to impose his or her views on the actors without real consultation. In the improvisation the director will voice his or her views but the actors will resist them. The aim of the improvisation should be to treat dramatically the issues raised by the Callow extract. If you like, you could have someone playing the playwright who wrote the play. How would the dramatist react to the conflict?

In the remainder of this chapter, four play extracts have been chosen to illustrate various aspects of writing for the theatre and the challenges each of these 'representative' plays face actors and directors with.

As in the rest of the book, each extract is prefaced by comment and some brief information about the playwright, the play from which the extract is taken, and notes on the salient characteristics that have made the extract an appropriate choice for our purposes. After each extract there is further comment and analysis and then suggestions for practical activities which will involve you in working on the text in an acting or directing role.

Realism on stage: Henrik Ibsen, *A Doll's House*

It was mentioned in 1.2 that nineteenth-century theatre was largely given over to spectacle and sentimental melodrama in Britain, certainly in Victorian times. Eventually there was a reaction against this and dramatists in various European countries set out to give the theatre a new direction. Henrik Ibsen (1828–1906), a Norwegian dramatist, has had a wide influence on twentieth-century drama, mainly because he was one of the writers who brought a new 'realism' to the stage. Realism in drama rejects theatricality (such as shock effects, dramatic twists and unlikely plots), and mainly deals with the lives of ordinary people in credible situations. Realism, unlike naturalism which we will look at in 3.2, does not set out to reproduce 'real life' on stage, but it does aim to reflect and comment on real life and social issues. Among the issues Ibsen deals with in his plays are municipal corruption, marriage and the family, and the position of women in society. Within these dramas about middle-class people he explores with psychological realism the motivations of individuals within the structure of society.

Below is an extract from one of Ibsen's best known plays, *A Doll's House* (1879).

> *A bell rings in the entryway; shortly after we hear the door being unlocked.* NORA *comes into the room, humming happily to herself; she is wearing street clothes and carries an armload of packages, which she puts down on the table to the right. She has left the hall door open; and through it a* DELIVERY BOY *is seen, holding a Christmas tree and a basket, which he gives to the* MAID *who lets them in.*

NORA	Hide the tree well, Helene. The children mustn't get a glimpse of it till this evening, after it's trimmed. (*to the* DELIVERY BOY, *taking out her purse*) How much?
DELIVERY BOY	Fifty, ma'am.
NORA	There's a crown. No, keep the change. (*The* BOY *thanks her and leaves.* NORA *shuts the door. She laughs softly to herself while taking off her street things. Drawing a bag of macaroons from her pocket, she eats a couple, then steals over and listens at her husband's study door.*) Yes, he's home. (*hums again as she moves to the table right*)
HELMER	(*from the study*) Is that my little lark twittering out there?
NORA	(*busy opening some packages*) Yes, it is.
HELMER	Is that my squirrel rummaging around?
NORA	Yes!
HELMER	When did my squirrel get in?
NORA	Just now. (*putting the macaroon bag in her pocket and wiping her mouth*) Do come in, Torvald, and see what I've bought.

HELMER   Can't be disturbed. (*After a moment he opens the door and peers in, pen in hand.*) Bought, you say? All that there? Has the little spendthrift been out throwing money around again?

NORA   Oh, but Torvald, this year we really should let ourselves go a bit. It's the first Christmas we haven't had to economise.

HELMER   But you know we can't go squandering.

NORA   Oh yes, Torvald, we can squander a little now. Can't we? Just a tiny, wee bit. Now that you've got a big salary and are going to make piles and piles of money.

HELMER   Yes – starting New Year's. But then it's a full three months till the raise comes through.

NORA   Pooh! We can borrow that long.

HELMER   Nora! (*goes over and playfully takes her by the ear*) Are your scatterbrains off again? What if today I borrowed a thousand crowns, and you squandered them over Christmas week, and then on New Year's Eve a roof tile fell on my head, and I lay there –

NORA   (*putting her hand on his mouth*) Oh! Don't say such things!

HELMER   Yes, but what if it happened – then what?

NORA   If anything so awful happened, then it just wouldn't matter if I had debts or not.

HELMER   Well, but the people I'd borrowed from?

NORA   Them? Who cares about them! They're strangers.

HELMER   Nora, Nora, how like a woman! No, but seriously, Nora, you know what I think about that. No debts! Never borrow! Something of freedom's lost – and something of beauty, too – from a home that's founded on borrowing and debt. We've made a brave stand up to now, the two of us; and we'll go right on like that the little while we have to.

NORA   (*going toward the stove*) Yes, whatever you say, Torvald.

HELMER   (*following her*) Now, now, the little lark's wings mustn't droop. Come on, don't be a sulky squirrel. (*taking out his wallet*) Nora, guess what I have here.

NORA   (*turning quickly*) Money!
HELMER   There, see. (*hands her some notes*) Good grief, I
          know how costs go up in a house at
          Christmastime.
NORA   Ten – twenty – thirty – forty. Oh, thank you,
          Torvald; I can manage no end on this.
HELMER   You really will have to.

Comment and activities

Rehearsal

When directors rehearse a scene with actors they usually have to be
able to discuss with them what they want to communicate to the
audience from particular sections of the play. It is quite common to
break scenes down into smaller sections for rehearsal purposes. The
director can then concentrate in rehearsal on each of these sections,
discussing with the actors what needs to be drawn out from that
particular part of the play. This 'drawing out' could be the underlining of a particular theme of the play, or the motivation of one of the
characters, or establishing an important point about the relationship
between characters. The director might aim to create an atmosphere,
or emphasise some detail of plot.

Directors' rehearsal notes

Both actors and directors have to prepare for rehearsal. They have to
be very familiar with the text. Actors, of course, have to learn their
lines, but, just as importantly, they have to understand their roles
within the overall context of the play. A director should be able to
help them achieve this understanding and advise them on how to
translate this understanding into an actual interpretation and
performance.

The director should study the section before rehearsal and make
brief notes about what should be established or underlined in the
scene. The notes should include practical advice for the actors.

For example, for the scene from *A Doll's House*, a director's notes
might look like this (see opposite):

Opening to Act I
Establish Nora's childlike dependence on
Helmer – Helmer's patronising judgemental
attitude to his wife; tone as talking to
a child.

Movement:
   Nora – fluttery, anxious, acting like
        little girl out to please daddy.
   Helmer – slow, assured, mock-stern,
        indulging slightly little child/
        daughter.

Acting the scene

Actors interpreting the roles of Nora and Helmer have to establish
important points about the characters they are playing immediately
the play opens. In this scene they have an excellent opportunity to
contrast the two characters. In rehearsal the actors and director could
discuss how best to contrast:

   i) the tone of their voices in speaking to one another
   ii) their movements and gestures

▷   How, for example, do you think the actor playing Helmer should say the
    following lines?

    Is that my little lark twittering out there?

    But you know we can't go squandering.

▷   How would the actor playing Nora deliver these lines?

    Oh, yes, Torvald, we can squander a little now. Can't we? Just a
    tiny, wee bit.

The text gives enough guidance to actors about how to integrate
gesture and movement into their interpretation of their roles. These

should emerge naturally from their playing of the characters and not appear to be attached artificially to their performance. Thus, in this scene, the actor playing Helmer might want to establish his fatherly, patronising attitude to his wife. This approach would imply certain gestures and way of moving round the stage, and suggest things about how he might touch his wife during the scene. The actor playing Nora should 'play up' to this, establishing Nora's compliance with her husband's idea of her. Nora is playing a part for her husband; she plays the 'little lark' and the 'squirrel' to get what she wants.

Improvisation in rehearsal

In rehearsing a scene, it is sometimes useful to depart completely from the text of the play and concentrate on the theme or essential dramatic situation of the scene in the form of improvisation. The improvisation could take the form of improvising 'in character' a scene between the characters which does not actually appear in the play but which might throw light on their motivations and relationship; or the improvisation could involve quite different people involved in a similar situation to the one you are rehearsing in the play. Here are some suggestions for improvising in rehearsal, in preparation for acting out the scene between Nora and Helmer.

▷   Improvisation 'in character': act out a scene from their past when they have decided to get married and are discussing what kind of life they will have together and what their respective roles in the marriage will be.

▷   Not 'in character': act out a scene in which a male patronises a female by taking a superior attitude or assuming a greater knowledge or experience. You could improvise two versions of the scene: one in which the female goes along with this male patronage and a second version in which she resists.

1.4   The playwright, theatrical language and the audience

The essence of theatre is live performance taking place in front of an audience. The performance is not recorded on video tape or film and transmitted to a distant audience sitting in their own homes (we shall look at television drama in 4.1). Unlike film-makers or television producers, theatre directors cannot transport the action to real locations and take their audience with them. The action of the play is confined to the acting space, although an audience can be invited to use its imagination, suspend its disbelief, and accept that the action of the play is set in many different places.

To help the audience accept the illusion of reality that most theatrical performances depend on, all kinds of theatrical language (techniques other than just the actual words spoken; see 3.1) are available to playwrights, actors and directors. These include dance, mime, stylised movement, exaggerated gesture, costume, make-up, music and special effects. Often, however, plays employ a bare minimum of these theatrical means. Other productions use every facet of theatrical language available; this approach is sometimes referred to as 'total theatre'.

Keeping up the theatrical illusion or breaking it?

The phrase 'theatrical illusion' means the acceptance by an audience that what is taking place on stage is 'real'. The audience involve themselves in this illusion, accepting characters and stage action as real people and real events. An audience that is totally involved in a play will feel the same emotions as the characters and identify with them and their situation. In these circumstances, the illusion is complete. In the world of television soap opera, too, some viewers accept the illusion created by the makers of these programmes so completely that they think of the characters and places as 'real' and send letters addressed to the 'Crossroads Motel' or the 'Rovers' Return'.

However, not all playwrights or directors wish to maintain this illusion in the theatre. They may deliberately break through the illusion and remind audiences that they are not watching real life, but a performance, a play, a piece of drama in which actors are pretending to be real people. The object of breaking the illusion is to ask audiences to stand back from the action of the drama and examine their reactions to the issues raised by the piece of make-believe. They are denied the 'luxury' of losing themselves in the action and the characters and the emotions aroused by them.

The alienation effect

Bertolt Brecht, a German playwright (1898-1956), was the first to use the term 'alienation effect' in relation to plays in the theatre. Brecht, a very politically-motivated playwright, believed that audiences should be confronted by contemporary political issues and should not be granted the comfort of losing themselves in a dramatic story or in sympathy for the characters (see 4.4). 'Alienation' means that audiences are always made conscious of the make-believe nature of theatre: their intellects and judgement are exercised rather than their emotional sympathies. Actors are encouraged to stand outside their role and may address the audience directly.

Robert Bolt, *A Man for all Seasons*

Robert Bolt is a contemporary British playwright. His best known play, *A Man for all Seasons* (1960), uses alienation effects that Brecht himself would have at least partly approved of. Bolt wrote this about his play:

> I tried for a bold and beautiful verbal architecture, a story rather than a plot, and overtly theatrical means of switching from one locale to another. I also used the most notorious of the alienation devices, an actor who addresses the audience and comments on the action. But I had him address the audience in character, that is, from within the play.

Below is an extract from the beginning of *A Man for all Seasons*.

When the curtain rises, the set is in darkness but for a single spot which descends vertically upon the COMMON MAN, *who stands in front of a big property basket.*

COMMON MAN   It is perverse! To start a play made up of Kings and Cardinals in speaking costumes and intellectuals with embroidered mouths, with me.
If a King, or a Cardinal had done the prologue he'd have had the right materials. And an intellectual would have shown enough majestic meanings, coloured propositions, and closely woven liturgical stuff to dress the House of Lords! But this!
Is this a costume? Does this say anything? It barely covers one man's nakedness! A bit of black material to reduce Old Adam to the Common Man.
Oh, if they'd let me come on naked, I could have shown you something of my own.
Which would have told you without words –!
. . . Something I've forgotten . . . Old Adam's muffled up.

(*backing towards basket*) Well, for a proposition of my own, I need a costume. (*takes out and puts on the coat and hat of* STEWARD) Matthew! The Household Steward of Sir Thomas More! (*Lights come up swiftly on set. He takes from the basket five silver goblets, one larger than the others, and a jug with a lid, with which he furnishes the table. A burst of conversational merriment off; he pauses and indicates head of stairs.*) There's company to dinner. (*finishes business at table*)

All right! A COMMON MAN! A Sixteenth-Century Butler! (*He drinks from the jug.*) All right – the Six . . . (*Breaks off, agreeably surprised by the quality of the liquor, regards the jug respectfully and drinks again.*) The Sixteenth Century is the Century of the Common Man. (*puts down the jug*) Like all the other centuries. (*crossing right*) And that's my proposition. (*During the last part of the speech, voices off. Now, enter, at head of stairs,* SIR THOMAS MORE.)

STEWARD	That's Sir Thomas More.
MORE	The wine please, Matthew?
STEWARD	It's there, Sir Thomas.
MORE	(*looking into jug*) Is it good?
STEWARD	Bless you, sir! *I* don't know.
MORE	(*mildly*) Bless you too, Matthew. (*enter* RICH *at head of stairs*)
RICH	(*enthusiastically pursuing an argument*) But every man has his price!
STEWARD	(*contemptuous*) Master Richard Rich.
RICH	But yes! In money too.
MORE	(*gentle impatience*) No no no.
RICH	Or pleasure. Titles, women, bricks-and-mortar, there's always something.
MORE	Childish.
RICH	Well, in suffering, certainly.
MORE	(*interested*) Buy a man with suffering?
RICH	Impose suffering, and offer him – escape.
MORE	Oh. For a moment I thought you were being profound. (*gives cup to* RICH)
RICH	(*to* STEWARD) Good evening, Matthew.
STEWARD	(*snubbing*) 'Evening, sir.

Comment and activities

The Common Man and alienation devices

The Common Man, as the play begins, is spot-lit, standing beside a property basket. A property basket contains the theatrical props that are needed during a production. Having the prop basket visible to the audience is a deliberate alienation device to remind the audience they are watching a theatrical performance.

Bolt follows this visual alienation device by emphasising it in the Common Man's words, 'To start a play made up of . . .'. The intention is to remind the audience they are watching a play, not real life. The audience are invited to stand back from the action and observe in a more detached manner than is usual in the theatre. However, as Bolt states in his comments above, the Common Man talks in character (he assumes the guise of various characters during the play by dressing in several items from the prop basket). Brecht would probably have made the actor playing the Common Man step out of character altogether and address the audience as an actor.

▷   In this extract how else does the Common Man remind the audience that they are watching a play rather than 'real life'?

Acting the scene

When More and Rich enter, the Common Man becomes the Steward and slides in and out of character – one minute he is this representative figure (with whom the audience may or may not identify) and the next he is the Steward interacting with More and Rich. The actors playing More and Rich do not acknowledge or address the audience; they keep up the theatrical illusion; they stay in character and behave as though the audience were not there. Thus, there are two strands in the scene: firstly the alienation device of the Common Man, and secondly the action between More and Rich in which the Common Man is involved as the Steward. The actor playing the Common Man would have to consider how differently he would approach the two parts and how he would address the audience directly.

▷   Divide up into small groups with one person in each group acting as director. Discuss what kind of delivery the actor playing the Common Man would use in addressing the audience and how the changeover to his acting the Steward could be managed. Would this opening alienation device affect how More and Rich would be played?

▷   Try to have a small prop basket available and, at least, a coat and a hat. If

possible, start the scene with the Common Man standing under a spot-
light, then bring the lights up as the text indicates. After you have
rehearsed the scene, discuss what effect the lighting has on the scene.

1.5   The imagination of the audience

Theatrical illusion does depend to a great extent on the willingness of
an audience to use its imagination. The cinema and television are
more realistic and literal media than the theatre. In a film, for
example, if a battle scene is called for, the cameras go to an outdoor
location and film the enactment of the battle in full, realistic terms.
Battle scenes on stage, however, have to depend much more on
symbolism, theatrical effects and illusion, and, crucially, the co-oper-
ation of the audience in accepting the conventions of the theatre.

William Shakespeare, *Henry V*

In Shakespeare's time, theatres had no modern technology to help
the actors to stage elaborate battle scenes or any other kind of scene.
There were no sets as such, and very few props or costumes. Shakespeare and other dramatists of the time had a bare stage to work on,
the skills of the actors, their own talents and the audience's
imagination.

   In the prologue to one of the most famous of his history plays,
Henry V (completed c. 1599), Shakespeare uses the Chorus (a narrator or commentator on the action of the play) to highlight the limitations of the stage in recreating history on a grand scale, and calls on
the audience to use their imagination to flesh out the action. The
'wooden O' which the Chorus refers to is the theatre where Shakespeare's play was being performed.

> CHORUS   . . . Can this cockpit hold
> The vasty fields of France? or may we cram
> Within this wooden O the very casques
> That did affright the air at Agincourt?
> O pardon! since a crooked figure may
> Attest in little place a million;
> And let us, ciphers to this great account,
> On your imaginary forces work;
> Suppose within the girdle of these walls
> Are now confined the two mighty monarchies
> Whose high upreared and abutting fronts
> The perilous narrow ocean parts asunder;

Piece out our imperfections with your thoughts:
Into a thousand parts divide one man
And make imaginary puissance;
Think when we talk of horses, that you see them
Printing their proud hoofs in the receiving earth;
For 'tis your thoughts that now must deck our Kings,
Carry them here and there; jumping o'er times,
Turning th'accomplishment of many years
Into an hour-glass; for the which supply
Admit me chorus to this history;
Who, prologue-like, your humble patience pray,
Gently to hear, kindly to judge, our play.

Like Bolt in *A Man for all Seasons*, Shakespeare addresses the audience directly through a commentator, the Chorus. But unlike the
Common Man, the Chorus in *Henry V* never becomes involved in the
action of the play. The idea of the Chorus comes from classical Greek
drama which normally used a group of actors speaking chorally who
commented on the drama, informed the audience about action that
took place off-stage and expressed emotions about what was
happening.

In the Chorus's speech above, Shakespeare appears to be apologis-
ing for the shortcomings of the theatre. He cannot summon up a
battlefield on stage, or armies or horses. But in saying this, he is also
underlining one of the strengths of the theatre — its claim on the
imagination of the audience. The power of Shakespeare's language
summons up the battlefield of Agincourt. In inviting the audience to
'piece out our imperfections', Shakespeare is saying, 'Let's join
together to create an illusion, to accept that this bare stage is France,
is a battlefield, is peopled with vast armies. You must suspend your
disbelief.'

The blasted heath: William Shakespeare, *King Lear*

Shakespeare included in his plays many scenes that called for spectacle and suggested great events. His audiences expected that of
drama, but they were used to the power of the language and the skills
of the actors providing these great scenes for them.

In his tragedy *King Lear* (1604-8), an old king, having divided his
kingdom between two of his daughters, has quarrelled bitterly with
both of them. Accusing them of monstrous ingratitude, he leaves his
daughter Regan's house, and wanders onto wild barren heathland,
accompanied only by his Fool (a professional jester at his court). A

raging storm is in progress. Kent, who enters in the middle of the
scene, is a faithful henchman who has been banished by Lear and is
now in disguise.

Another part of the heath. Storm still. Enter LEAR *bare-headed with*
FOOL.

LEAR   Blow, winds, and crack your cheeks! rage! blow!
       You cataracts and hurricanoes, spout
       Till you have drenched our steeples, drowned the cocks!
       You sulph'rous and thought-executing fires,
       Vaunt-couriers of oak-cleaving thunderbolts,
       Singe my white head! And thou, all-shaking thunder,
       Strike flat the thick rotundity o'th'world,
       Crack Nature's moulds, all germens spill at once
       That make ingrateful man!
FOOL   O nuncle, court holy water in a dry house is better than
       this rain-water out o'door. Good nuncle, in; ask thy
       daughters blessing! Here's a night pities neither wise men
       nor fools.
LEAR   Rumble thy bellyful! Spit, fire! spout, rain!
       Nor rain, wind, thunder, fire are my daughters.
       I tax not you, you elements, with unkindness:
       I never gave you kingdom, called you children;
       You owe me no subscription. Then let fall
       Your horrible pleasure. Here I stand, your slave,
       A poor, infirm, weak, and despised old man:
       But yet I call you servile ministers,
       That will with two pernicious daughters join
       Your high-engendered battles 'gainst a head
       So old and white as this. O, ho! 'tis foul!
FOOL   He that has a house to put's head in has a good head-
       piece.
                    The codpiece that will house
                    Before the head has any,
                    The head and he shall louse:
                    So beggars marry many.
                    The man that makes his toe
                    What he his heart should make
                    Shall of a corn cry woe,
                    And turn his sleep to wake.
       For there was never yet fair woman but she made mouths
       in a glass.
       (*enter* KENT)

LEAR   No, I will be the pattern of all patience; I will say
       nothing.
KENT   Who's there?
FOOL   Marry, here's grace and a codpiece; that's a wise man and
       (*pointing at* LEAR) a fool.
KENT   Alas, sir, are you here? Things that love night
       Love not such nights as these. The wrathful skies
       Gallow the very wanderers of the dark
       And make them keep their caves. Since I was man,
       Such sheets of fire, such bursts of horrid thunder,
       Such groans of roaring wind and rain, I never
       Remember to have heard. Man's nature cannot carry
       Th'affliction nor the fear.
LEAR   Let the great gods,
       That keep this dreadful pudder o'er our heads,
       Find out their enemies now. Tremble, thou wretch
       That hast within thee undivulgéd crimes
       Unwhipped of justice. Hide thee, thou bloody hand,
       Thou perjured, and thou simular of virtue
       That art incestuous. Caitiff, to pieces shake,
       That under covert and convenient seeming
       Hast practised on man's life. Close pent-up guilts,
       Rive your concealing continents, and cry
       These dreadful summoners grace. I am a man
       More sinned against than sinning.
KENT   Alack, bare-headed?
       Gracious my lord, hard by here is a hovel; Some
       friendship will it lend you 'gainst the tempest:
       Repose you there, while I to this hard house
       (More harder than the stone whereof 'tis raised,
       Which even but now, demanding after you,
       Denied me to come in) return, and force
       Their scanted courtesy.
LEAR   My wits begin to turn.
       Come on, my boy. How dost, my boy? Art cold?
       I am cold myself. Where is this straw, my fellow?
       The art of our necessities is strange,
       And can make vile things precious. Come, your hovel.
       Poor fool and knave, I have one part in my heart
       That's sorry yet for thee.
FOOL   (*sings*)
             He that has and a little tiny wit,
                With heigh-ho, the wind and the rain,

>   Must make content with his fortunes fit,
>   Though the rain it raineth every day.
> LEAR True, boy. Come, bring us to this hovel.
>   (LEAR *and* KENT *go.*)

Comment and Activities

Producing the storm

Most modern productions of *King Lear* employ a battery of effects to represent the storm in this scene. There are usually sounds of thunder produced by vast thunder sheets backstage or through audio tape, lightning effects, the howling of the wind, the sound of the downpour. However, a balance has to be found between the theatrical effects and the delivery of the verse by the actors. If the sound and lighting effects overwhelm the actors, the scene will be swamped with technological overkill. It is the director's responsibility to use these effects in the service of the dramatic situation and to help the actors.

Effects like those described above can usually be established at the beginning of a scene, then used sparingly until an opportune time in the drama allows the director to 'bring them up' again.

A production script for the start of this scene might look like this:

Scene 2   Heath

> *Thunder sheet: three very loud rolls followed by two lesser; lightning effect; sound of rain.*
> *Enter* LEAR *and* FOOL. *They struggle in storm. Howling of wind emphasised.*
>
> LEAR Blow, winds, and crack you cheeks! rage! blow!

This production script calls for the ferocity of the storm to be established right at the beginning of the scene. Then, having established this, the sound effects are 'brought down' so that the actor playing Lear can be heard as he shouts his first speech against the noise of the storm. A director, however, is likely to find other places in the text where storm effects could be used to remind the audience of the full impact of the tempest.

▷   In small groups discuss the scene and decide where and how you could use storm effects and how you think the actors should react to them on stage.

Acting the scene

Again there is an excellent chance of contrast between the actors in
this scene. The deranged old man hurling defiance at the storm can be
contrasted with the Fool, intent on survival and urging the King to beg
his daughters' forgiveness. Both of these attitudes contrast with the
solid, good sense of the reliable Kent.

Lear, however, goes through several emotional changes in this
scene and an actor playing the role would have to communicate this.
To begin with he is declamatory, then 'the pattern of all patience';
after that he appears insane in his accusations of corruption and
gentle in his concern for the Fool. His varying moods find expression
in the text and the actor must vary his delivery accordingly. Similarly,
there is the opportunity for the actor playing the Fool to use variation
and contrast.

▷   Rehearse this scene in groups, looking for ways to vary delivery of the
     lines. Once you have rehearsed the text, add sound and other effects to
     enhance the dramatic impact of the scene.

1.6   Whose play is it anyway?

Does a play 'belong' to the playwright who wrote it? Plays are always
advertised as being 'by' a particular author: King Lear by William
Shakespeare; A Man for all Seasons by Robert Bolt. But what happens to that play, the text, when it is delivered into the hands of a
director and actors for rehearsal and eventual performance?

Contemporary dramatists sometimes sit in on rehearsals of their
plays, but it is generally accepted that the writer takes a back seat and
leaves it to the director and actors to translate the text into performance. The majority of actors and directors acknowledge their
responsibility to the text as written by the dramatist and see their task
as being to interpret the playwright's intentions as faithfully as
possible.

Re-interpreting the text

However, some actors and directors do not share this view of the text
as 'sacred'. Usually it is a director with a particular concept of a play
who is responsible for the re-interpetation of a play text or even
radically altering the structure of the play by re-ordering scenes,
cutting dialogue, introducing theatrical devices and stage business
that do not appear in the original script. It is this kind of interpretation that has given rise to the term 'directors' theatre': the director as

the most important creative influence on a production, more important than the dramatist who provides the text (see 1.3).

Generally, it is plays by dead playwrights that receive the benefit of directorial genius in this way – after all, dead playwrights cannot protect the text. But occasionally disputes arise between contemporary dramatists and theatre companies about the interpretation plays receive. Then the question of the 'ownership' of a play arises.

The tradition of the *commedia dell'arte:* Dario Fo, *Accidental Death of an Anarchist*

Dario Fo is a contemporary Italian performer, director and writer who believes in taking drama out of the established theatres to places where 'ordinary' people meet and work: factories, community halls, open-air festivals and indeed anywhere there is a practical performing space. The roots of the kind of popular theatre Fo likes are in the 'knockabout comedies' which groups of travelling players used to perform in the middle ages, and the *commedia dell'arte* which developed in Italy in the sixteenth century (which, like knockabout comedy, used caricature, buffoonery, mime, farcical situations and stock characters). The 'plays' which the *commedia dell'arte* actors performed grew out of improvisation in rehearsal.

Fo has his own travelling theatre company and it mounts shows that are created in rehearsal by Fo and the other performers. However, Fo is also a dramatist. In his play, *Accidental Death of an Anarchist* (1970), Fo uses the genre of farce and the traditions of caricature and buffoonery, and knockabout comedy, to deal satirically with a tragic event with strong political overtones.

An interesting question arose following the London production of Fo's play in 1980. The director and actors based their production on an adaptation from the Italian into English. The dramatist later protested, however, at the way in which the play was interpreted on stage. This fuelled discussion in theatre circles about whether dramatists have proprietary rights over their plays, or whether the interpretation of the play is the responsibility of director and actors.

Below is an extract from the play. A bomb has exploded in an Italian bank, killing sixteen people. Anarchists are blamed for the outrage. A man is arrested and questioned by the police. During the course of the interrogation the suspect is supposed to have thrown himself out of the fourth-floor window of the police headquarters. The police claim his death was suicide.

Eventually it is established that the suspect had nothing to do with

the planting of the bomb. The action of the play deals with the
cover-up undertaken by the authorities as they try to conceal the
truth of the affair. In this extract, the Maniac, disguised as an inves-
tigating magistrate, is questioning a policeman involved in the interrogation of the suspect. Pisani is a police inspector.

MANIAC	Set the scene.
CONSTABLE	(*hesitant*) Er ... it's midnight ...
	(MANIAC *makes an owl noise. Others help*
	create midnight atmosphere.)
	... there are five of us in this room ... the
	suspect, myself, and another constable and
	...
SUPERINTENDANT	... I'd just stepped out ...
MANIAC	Sssh!
CONSTABLE	And ... er ...
MANIAC	Those two?
CONSTABLE	Yes.
	(PISANI *glares at* CONSTABLE.)
MANIAC	What are they doing?
CONSTABLE	Interrogating the suspect.
MANIAC	Still? After all these hours? Must be
	knackered?
	'Where were you on the night of ...?'
	'Don't play dumb with me' on and on, dear
	God but you must be exasperated.
PISANI	Just a bit.
MANIAC	I expect you fancy roughing him up a bit?
PISANI	Never touched the bastard.
SUPERINTENDANT	Very even tempered. The whole
	proceedings.
MANIAC	Don't get me wrong.
	Just a little slap, pchew!, across the chops?
PISANI	Never got near him.
MANIAC	Bit of a massage, to relieve his tensions ...
	(MANIAC *starts to massage* CONSTABLE.)
	... shoulders full of cramps
	... yes ...
CONSTABLE	Left a bit.
MANIAC	Left a bit. There.
CONSTABLE	Lovely.
MANIAC	... After all those hours ... and then ...

	(*sudden karate chop*)
	... Ka ...
	(*karate act*)
	... Ka! Ya! Eeeaaah!
PISANI	(*very indignant*) There was no violence, no massage, no karate, nothing like that. It was all above board according to regulations. We were conducting our enquiries in a very lighthearted manner.
MANIAC	You *were* interrogating him?
PISANI	Lightheartedly.
SUPERINTENDANT	We were having a bit of laugh with him.
MANIAC	Playing 'Grandmother's footsteps' were you? Paper hats? Stick the tail on the donkey?
CONSTABLE	It was just the odd joke, your Honour, you should see the Inspector when he's on form. Hilarious. Keeps us all in stitches. Ha ha.
MANIAC	Especially when interrogating mass murder suspects.
CONSTABLE	Especially then. Ha, Er ...
MANIAC	So you're a bit of a wag, Inspector.
PISANI	Well ...
MANIAC	Don't be modest. Take the stage, give us a quick dose.
CONSTABLE	Go on sir.
	(PISANI *tells jokes. Takes applause.*)
MANIAC	Did you tell the suspect that one?
PISANI	Yes.
MANIAC	No wonder he jumped.

Comment and Activities

Fo provides many opportunities in the text for the actors to use their comic talents. He indicates what he wants:

(MANIAC *makes an owl noise. Others help create midnight atmosphere.*)

(*Karate act*)

(PISANI *tells jokes. Takes applause.*)

These brief stage directions give plenty of scope for invention on the part of actors and directors.

Notice how much opportunity there is for physical action and knockabout arising from the text. Fo's play is a manual for performance. However, there are satirical and serious elements too.

Acting the scene

▷ In small groups, discuss what kind of physical action is required for the performance of this scene. For example, practise the creating of a 'midnight atmosphere', the karate act and the joke-telling act.

▷ In addition to these opportunities, there are other instances in the text where knockabout action is required. Rehearse the scene, then act it out, concentrating not only on bringing out the comic elements but also on emphasising the 'serious' issues involved as well.

▷ Discuss the question of whether a dramatist 'owns' the play he or she has written. Do actors and directors owe their first loyalty to the text and the intentions of the dramatist, or have they the absolute right to re-interpret the text exactly as they wish?

▷ After discussing these issues, improvise a scene in which a playwright is sitting in on a rehearsal of a play he or she has written. In the playwright's view the actors and director begin to 'take liberties' with the text. The playwright objects to this. Arguments about the ownership of the play ensue …

1.7   Checklist and further resources

The following terms and ideas have been used and discussed in this chapter. Check through the list and make sure you know the meaning of each of them. If you are uncertain about any of them, read through the relevant sections of the chapter again and/or check the glossary at the end of the book.

theatrical language   realism
alternative theatre   theatricality
fringe theatre   improvisation
proscenium arch   theatrical illusion
thrust stage   alienation effect
arena stage   property basket
theatre-in-the-round   re-interpreting the text

open stage   *commedia dell'arte*
commercial theatre   knockabout
subsidised theatre   caricature
'formula' plays   buffoonery
directors' theatre   stock characters
company style

For another example of realism, a scene from Granville Barker's play *Waste* (1907) could be studied.

A film version of Ibsen, *A Doll's House*, starring Jane Fonda is available on video.

A film version of Bolt, *A Man for all Seasons*, starring Paul Schofield as Thomas More is available on video.

King Lear starring Laurence Olivier in a television production is also available on video.

2 The openings to plays

2.1 The audience's attention

Think about occasions when you have gone to the theatre. You sit in your seat waiting expectantly for the performance to begin. The house lights go down, the stage lights come up and the performance starts. These are vital moments for the dramatist and the performers. As a member of an audience, your attention is either engaged during these opening moments or it is not. If you are not 'hooked' by the beginning of the play, then the dramatist and the performers will find it hard to make you warm to the rest.

Exposition

Part of engaging that interest is informing the audience what the play is about, who the characters are, what the dramatic situation is and when and where the action on stage is supposed to be taking place. Playwrights must attempt to convey this essential information in dramatic terms: in words and action that are integrated completely with the drama. Heavy-handed and intrusive scene-setting has to be avoided.

Most plays require some exposition, and it is a measure of the dramatist's skill how subtly it is done. For examples of unsubtle scene-setting, some Hollywood 'period' films are a warning to all writers: the film makers are intent on establishing period and setting at all costs. Here is an example:

> The scene is set in nineteenth-century London. The film opens on a foggy street; an organ-grinder is seen and heard; hansom cabs pass to and fro and a London bobby strolls by. Two top-hatted gentlemen meet, raise their hats and say, 'Good morning, Mr Dickens' and, 'Ah, good morning, Mr Thackeray'.

Scene-setting with a vengeance!

Selectivity

A play in the theatre usually lasts between two and three hours. A playwright generally cannot be as expansive as a novelist. The selection of dramatic incident, the number of important characters, the themes to be dealt with and the dialogue to be spoken, must be chosen with extreme care. Every dramatic incident and strand of the plot must contribute meaningfully to the play. Every character must add something of significance to the drama. Every line of text must pay its way in dramatic terms. The playwright has to have a selective ear and an instinct for what will work dramatically. He or she must also have an economic style of writing.

Hence, in part, the importance of the beginnings of plays. If the exposition is too complex and long-winded, if the plot seems tangled, if the number of characters who have to be introduced is too many or the underlying themes of the play remain obscure, then an audience will quickly become confused, dissatisfied and bored.

John Galsworthy, *Strife*

John Galsworthy was a well-known novelist in the early twentieth century who also wrote a number of successful plays. They are conventional three-act plays, written to be performed on proscenium arch stages. He was probably much influenced as a dramatist by Ibsen's brand of stage realism (see 1.3) – his plays confront social issues of his day and explore the moral questions at the heart of conflict in society.

His play *Strife* (1909) deals with the issue of industrial unrest. In the opening minutes of the play Galsworthy has to communicate to the audience basic information about the dramatic situation, about the relationships between the characters on stage and some of the attitudes they have towards the strikers. This provides a complex problem of exposition.

The action at the opening of the play takes place in Underwood's dining-room where a bright fire is burning. Anthony is sitting at the head of a long table, in the Chairman's place. Edgar is reading a newspaper; Wanklin is bending over some papers and Tench and Underwood are beside him. Wilder is standing in front of, and Scantlebury has his back to, the fire.

WILDER	(*who is lean, cadaverous, and complaining, with drooping grey moustaches, stands before the fire.*) I say, this fire's the devil! Can I have a screen, Tench?
SCANTLEBURY	A screen, ah!
TENCH	Certainly, Mr Wilder. (*He looks at* UNDERWOOD.) That is – perhaps the Manager – perhaps Mr Underwood . . .

SCANTLEBURY	These fireplaces of yours, Underwood . . .
UNDERWOOD	(*roused from studying some papers*) A screen? Rather! I'm sorry. (*He goes to the door with a little smile.*) We're not accustomed to complaints of too much fire down here just now. (*He speaks as though he holds a pipe between his teeth, slowly, ironically.*)
WILDER	(*in an injured voice*) You mean the men. H'm! (UNDERWOOD *goes out.*)
SCANTLEBURY	Poor devils!
WILDER	It's their own fault, Scantlebury.
EDGAR	(*holding out his paper*) There's great distress amongst them, according to the *Trenartha News*.
WILDER	Oh, that rag! Give it to Wanklin. Suit his Radical views. They call us monsters, I suppose. The editor of that rubbish ought to be shot.
EDGAR	(*reading*) 'If the Board of worthy gentlemen who control the Trenartha Tin Plate Works from their armchairs in London, would condescend to come and see for themselves the conditions prevailing amongst their workpeople during this strike. . .'
WILDER	Well, we *have* come.
EDGAR	(*continuing*) 'We cannot believe that even their leg-of-mutton hearts would remain untouched.' (WANKLIN *takes the paper from him.*)
WILDER	Ruffian! I remember that fellow when he hadn't a penny to his name; little snivel of a chap that's made his way by blackguarding everybody who takes a different view to himself. (ANTHONY *says something that is not heard*)
WILDER	What does your father say?
EDGAR	He says 'The kettle and the pot'.
WILDER	H'm! (*He sits down next to* SCANTLEBURY.)
SCANTLEBURY	(*blowing out his cheeks*) I shall boil if I don't get that screen. (UNDERWOOD *and* ENID *enter with a screen, which they place before the fire.* ENID *is tall; she has a small, decided face, and is twenty-eight years old.*)
ENID	Put it closer, Frank. Will that do, Mr. Wilder? It's the highest we've got.
WILDER	Thanks, capitally.
SCANTLEBURY	*turning, with a sigh of pleasure*) Ah! Merci, Madame!
ENID	Is there anything else you want, father?

	(ANTHONY *shakes his head.*) Edgar – anything?
EDGAR	You might give me a 'J' nib, old girl.
ENID	There are some down there by Mr Scantlebury.
SCANTLEBURY	(*handing a little box of nibs*) Ah! your brother uses 'J's'. What does the manager use? (*with expansive politeness*) What does your husband use, Mrs Underwood?
UNDERWOOD	A quill!
SCANTLEBURY	The homely product of the goose. (*He holds out quills.*)
UNDERWOOD	(*dryly*) Thanks, if you can spare me one. (*He takes a quill.*) What about lunch, Enid?
ENID	(*stopping at the double doors and looking back*) We're going to have lunch here, in the drawing-room, so you needn't hurry with your meeting. (WANKLIN *and* WILDER *bow, and she goes out.*)
SCANTLEBURY	(*rousing himself, suddenly*) Ah! Lunch! That hotel – dreadful! Did you try the whitebait last night? Fried fat!
WILDER	Past twelve! Aren't you going to read the minutes, Tench?
TENCH	(*looking for the* CHAIRMAN's *assent, reads in a rapid and monotonous voice*) 'At a Board Meeting held the 31st of January at the Company's Offices, 512, Cannon Street, E.C. Present – Mr Anthony in the chair, Messrs F. H. Wilder, William Scantlebury, Oliver Wanklin, and Edgar Anthony. Read letters from the Manager dated January 20th, 23rd, 25th 28th, relative to the strike at the Company's Works. Read letters to the Manager of January 21st, 24th, 26th, 29th. Read letter from Mr Simon Harness, of the Central Union, asking for an interview with the Board. Read letter from the Men's Committee, signed David Roberts, James Green, John Bulgin, Henry Thomas, George Rous, desiring conference with the Board; and it was resolved that a special Board Meeting be called for February at the house of the Manager, for the purpose of discussing the situation with Mr Simon Harness and the Men's Committee on the spot. Passed twelve transfers, signed and sealed nine certificates and one balance certificate.' (*He pushes the book over to the* CHAIRMAN.)

ANTHONY   (*with a heavy sigh*) If it's your pleasure, sign the
               same.
               (*He signs, moving the pen with difficulty.*)
WANKLIN   What's the Union's game, Tench? They haven't
               made up their split with the men. What does
               Harness want this interview for?
TENCH   Hoping we shall come to a compromise, I think,
               sir; he's having a meeting with the men this
               afternoon.
WILDER   Harness! Ah! He's one of those cold-blooded
               cool-headed chaps. I distrust them. I don't know
               that we didn't make a mistake to come down.
               What time'll the men be here?
UNDERWOOD   Any time now.
WILDER   Well, if we're not ready, they'll have to wait –
               won't do 'em any harm to cool their heels a bit.
SCANTLEBURY   (*slowly*) Poor devils! It's snowing; *What* weather!

Comment and activities

A director's rehearsal notes for this opening section might look like
this:

> Establish facts about strike — make
> quote from newspaper and reading of
> minutes very clear; emphasise important
> details.
> Establish characters / conflict of attitudes
> Wilder: anti-strikes, vindictive; Scantlebury:
> fairly sympathetic.
> Establish name of Harness with audience.

The director's task is to guide the actors to communicate the necessary exposition in a natural, unforced manner. The information should be communicated through the interaction between characters.

Exposition through theatrical means

For the purposes of exposition Galsworthy uses these ploys:
- ○ the reading of a newspaper editorial commenting on the strike
- ○ the reading of minutes of a committee meeting that records matters to do with the strike
- ○ questions and answers between characters

Harness' name is mentioned twice: once in the reading of the minutes and once by Wanklin who asks Tench what Harness is up to. This establishes the name of the character with the audience and they will expect to see him on stage before long.

Acting the scene

The director will need to remind the actors about which essential facts need to be emphasised and clearly spoken. The names of the characters should be stressed – this can be done through pauses and variation of the pitch of the voice. There are important characters and facts that have to be established. In addition, the actors have to establish in these opening minutes the outlines of their own characters.

▷   Each of you should make your own director's notes on the scene. Briefly write down notes about essential exposition which you think needs to be communicated to the audience. Add some details about what you would like to establish about each of the characters.

▷   Then divide into groups and compare the notes you have made on the scene with those made by other group members. Rehearse the scene, with one of you taking the role of director, paying specific attention to establishing characters and to clear, but not heavy-handed, exposition.

2.2   Creating a mood and establishing themes

In the opening minutes of a play the dramatist, aided by the director and the actors, can aim to create an atmosphere, a mood, and alert the audience to some of the themes the play is going to deal with. As with exposition, the creating of atmosphere and the establishment of themes can be handled in either a subtle or heavy-handed manner, depending on the skill of the dramatist and the performers.

Anton Chekhov, *Three Sisters*

Chekhov was a Russian dramatist who was writing his plays at about the same time as Ibsen. Like Ibsen he wanted to introduce a new realism to his country's drama. However, Chekhov's realism is a very atmospheric brand compared to the more literal realism of Ibsen.

Chekhov has had an enormous influence on European drama and it has not always been a beneficial influence. This is because less-talented writers have tried to imitate the 'Chekhovian' evocation of mood and themes and have failed because they lack his dramatic skills and understanding of people. Chekhov was a master-craftsman; he had the ability to create an atmosphere in his plays and portray a picture of a society in decline (pre-revolutionary Russia), in drama that audiences ever since have found compelling and moving.

Below is the opening section from Chekhov's play *Three Sisters* (1901). The three sisters are Olga, Irena and Masha.

> *A drawing-room in the Prozorovs' house; it is separated from a large ballroom at the back by a row of columns. It is midday; there is cheerful sunshine outside. In the ballroom the table is being laid for lunch.* OLGA, *wearing the regulation dark-blue dress of a secondary school mistress, is correcting her pupils' work, standing or walking about as she does so.* MASHA, *in a black dress, is sitting reading a book, her hat on her lap.* IRENA, *in white, stands lost in thought.*

OLGA   It's exactly a year ago that Father died, isn't it? This very day, the fifth of May – your Saint's day, Irena. I remember it was very cold and it was snowing. I felt then as if I should never survive his death; and you had fainted and were lying quite still, as if you were dead. And now – a year's gone by, and we talk about it so easily. You're wearing white, and your face is positively radiant . . .
(*a clock strikes twelve.*)
The clock struck twelve then, too. (*a pause*) I remember when Father was being taken to the cemetery there was a military band, and a salute with rifle fire. That was because he was a general, in command of a brigade. And yet there weren't many people at the funeral. Of course, it was raining hard, raining and snowing.

IRENA   Need we bring up all these memories?
(BARON TOOZENBACH, CHEBUTYKIN *and*

SOLIONY *appear behind the columns by the table in the ballroom.*)

OLGA   It's so warm today that we can keep the windows wide open, and yet there aren't any leaves showing on the birch trees. Father was made a brigadier eleven years ago, and then he left Moscow and took us with him. I remember so well how everything in Moscow was in blossom by now, everything was soaked in sunlight and warmth. Eleven years have gone by, yet I remember everything about it, as if we'd only left yesterday. Oh, Heavens! When I woke up this morning and saw this flood of sunshine, all this spring sunshine, I felt so moved and so happy! I felt such a longing to get back home to Moscow!

CHEBUTYKIN   (*to* TOOZENBACH) The devil you have!

TOOZENBACH   It's nonsense, I agree.

MASHA   (*absorbed in her book, whistles a tune under her breath*)

OLGA   Masha, do stop whistling! How can you? (*a pause*) I suppose I must get this continual headache because I have to go to school every day and go on teaching right into the evening. I seem to have the thoughts of someone quite old. Honestly, I've been feeling as if my strength and youth were running out of me drop by drop, day after day. Day after day, all these four years that I've been working at the school ... I just have one longing and it seems to grow stronger and stronger ...

IRENA   If only we could go back to Moscow! Sell the house, finish with our life here, and go back to Moscow.

OLGA   Yes, Moscow! As soon as we possibly can.
(CHEBUTYKIN *and* TOOZENBACH *laugh.*)

IRENA   I suppose Andrey will soon get a professorship. He isn't likely to go on living here. The only problem is our poor Masha.

OLGA   Masha can come and stay the whole summer with us every year in Moscow.

MASHA   (*whistles a tune under her breath*)

IRENA   Everything will settle itself, with God's help. (*looks through the window*) What lovely weather it is today! Really, I don't know why there's such joy in my heart. I remembered this morning that it was my Saint's day, and suddenly I felt so happy, and I thought of the time when we were children, and Mother was still alive. And then such wonderful thoughts came to me, such wonderful stirring thoughts!

OLGA   You're so lovely today, you really do look most attractive. Masha looks pretty today, too. Andrey could be good-looking, but he's grown so stout. It doesn't suit him. As for me, I've just aged and grown a lot thinner. I suppose it's through getting so irritated with the girls at school. But today I'm at home, I'm free, and my headache's gone, and I feel much younger than I did yesterday. I'm only twenty-eight, after all . . . I suppose everything that God wills must be right and good, but I can't help thinking sometimes that if I'd got married and stayed at home, it would have been a better thing for me. (*a pause*) I would have been very fond of my husband.

TOOZENBACH (*to* SOLIONY) Really, you talk such a lot of nonsense, I'm tired of listening to you. (*comes into the drawing-room*) I forgot to tell you: Vershinin, our new battery commander, is going to call on you today. (*sits down by the piano*)

OLGA   I'm very glad to hear it.

Comment and activities

Mood and Themes

Immediately the play starts Chekhov plunges us into the lives of his characters. We hear Olga recalling that the sisters' father died a year ago and that he was a general in the army. Behind the women on stage, three army officers in uniform enter, so the military connection is continued in the minds of the audience. Irena, 'lost in thought', resists dwelling on sad memories, but Olga continues to reminisce: she mentions the bare birch trees in comparison with 'Moscow in bloom'. The present sunshine makes her recall their happy life in Moscow and her longing to return there.

Already in these opening minutes Chekhov has told us important facts about the situation of his main characters. He has established a mood (regret for a past life and a feeling of waiting for something to happen), and has suggested a theme (frustrated desire to experience another kind of life).

Chekhov often has his characters tell the audience directly from their own mouths facts about themselves; they also express their feelings very directly:

> OLGA   ... I seem to have the thoughts of someone quite old. Honestly, I've been feeling as though my strength and youth were running out of me drop by drop, day after day
> ...
>
> IRENA   If only we could get back to Moscow! Sell the house, finish with our life here, and go back to Moscow.

Masha says nothing in this opening scene, but the audience should be very aware of her brooding presence. She is reading but whistles under her breath when Olga is talking about returning to Moscow. Her silence and her repressed irritation should make a strong impression on an audience.

Pacing a scene

One important task the director and actors have to take on is how a scene should be 'paced'. If the pace of a scene is uniform throughout, then it will be monotonous. There must be a variation in pace and these variations should arise from the dramatic situations. The scene above is dominated by three longish speeches by Olga. They are interspersed by short speeches by Irena, by Masha's whistling and by snatches of conversation from the officers in the background. These provide breaks in Olga's flow of speech. The director and actors have to integrate these into the action and allow for pauses.

Delivering long speeches

Chekhov is a master at writing long speeches for actors. He allows for changes in pace, pauses, stresses and variations of tone. All this is evident in the text, but an actor preparing to play Olga in this scene would have to analyse the speeches in detail and note how she could achieve variation in her vocal delivery to match the changing moods of the character.

Here is an example of how Olga's first speech could be 'broken down' by an actor playing her (see overleaf):

OLGA   It is exactly a year ago that Father died, isn't it? This very

day, the fifth of May – your Saint's day, Irena. I remember
Turning to Irena 'recalling' tone

it was very cold and it was snowing. I felt then I should

never survive his death; and you had fainted and were lying

quite still, as if you were dead./And now – a year's gone by
Pause   new animation,

and we talk about it so easily. You're wearing white and
quieter delivery   expressing pleasure

your face is positively radiant . . . (*A clock strikes twelve.*) A

clock struck twelve then, too.   *Pause:*
recalling sadly   silence

You can see how Chekhov has written a speech of changing moods
and emphases. The actor, to be true to the text and the playwright's
intentions, needs to follow these variations.

▷   Analyse the other two main speeches by Olga in this scene and work on
how they could be delivered using a variation of tone, emphasis and
pace. Where could pauses be used for dramatic effect? How could the
pitch of the voice be varied?

Acting the scene

▷   Rehearse the scene in a group with a director. Concentrate on how you
pace the scene and establish themes and mood for the audience. Look
for ways to vary the delivery and how characters could be established in
these opening minutes of the play. Chekhov has provided plenty of
'clues' in the text for the actors and directors.

2.3   Intriguing openings

There is an old show business adage about 'socking it to them from the moment the curtain rises'. If that advice is followed, musicals start with a lively and elaborate 'audience-hooking' production number; thrillers start with the discovery of the murdered body; comedies have a few sure-fire gags that set the audience off laughing. That is the theory, anyway.

'Serious' plays usually use less flamboyant means to 'hook' their audience. Sometimes, however, some kind of *coup de théâtre* is employed. *Coup de théâtre* is a term for a theatrical happening that startles or involves the audience in an unexpected manner. For example, in Peter Shaffer's play *Black Comedy* (1965), the actors start the scene (set in a flat) in darkness – the stage is dark as far as the audience are concerned but the actors (and therefore the characters they are playing) carry on as though the lights were on. The audience cannot see the actors but can only hear their voices. After a few minutes, the stage lights come on and the audience can see the actors for the first time. For the characters in the play, though, the reverse has happened. As far as they are concerned the lighting has fused in the flat, they have been plunged into darkness and they have to blunder their way around the stage. Here the *coup de théâtre* lies in the startling effect of the light-dark reversal. When the characters are in the dark from the audience's point of view, they behave as normal; when the audience can see the action on stage, the characters behave as though they were in complete darkness. It is a very clever theatrical effect.

Caryl Churchill, *Top Girls*

The first act of Caryl Churchill's *Top Girls* (1982) has a similarly intriguing effect on an audience. The playwright has created a dramatic situation in which famous women from various historical periods meet in a present-day restaurant. Each character is dressed in a costume from the time in which they were alive and which denotes what they were famous for.

The intriguing theatrical effect for the audience lies in the incongruity of the mix of characters – from real historical figures to characters from fiction and mythology. The contemporary setting is also incongruous, chosen by the hostess, a Managing Director of an Employment Agency, who has arranged the dinner to celebrate her promotion to that position.

As well as the hostess, the other 'Top Girls' are Isabella Bird (1831-1904), a Scottish explorer; Lady Nijo (born 1258), a Japanese cour-

Top Girls by Caryl Churchill: first produced at the Royal Court Theatre in London in 1982. The first scene of the play uses the intriguing device of characters in full period dress from different historical ages meeting in a contemporary restaurant.

tesan and later a Bhuddist nun; Dull Gret, an legendary Dutch female warrior of the middle ages; Pope Joan who, disguised as a man, is thought to have been Pope between 854 and 856; and Patient Griselda who was the obedient wife in the story told by Chaucer in the Clerk's Tale of the *Canterbury Tales*.

The extract below is from the beginning of the play. First though, a note on the layout of the script: usually a speech follows on naturally after the preceding speech in the text, but the dramatist in this play has indicated where she intends one character's speaking to overlap with another character's speaking (i.e. to start speaking before the other has finished). The point of interruption is marked /. Sometimes a speech follows on from a speech earlier than the one immediately before it and the continuity is marked ★.

> *Restaurant. Table set for dinner with white tablecloth. Six places.*
> MARLENE *and* WAITRESS.

> MARLENE   Excellent, yes, table for six. One of them's going to be
> late but we won't wait. I'd like a bottle of Frascati
> straight away if you've got one really cold.

(ISABELLA BIRD *arrives.*)
Here we are, Isabella.

ISABELLA   Congratulations, my dear.

MARLENE   Well, it's a step. It makes for a party. I haven't time for a holiday. I'd like to go somewhere exotic like you but I can't get away. I don't know how you could bear to leave Hawaii./I'd like to lie

ISABELLA   I did think of settling.

MARLENE   in the sun forever, except of course I can't bear sitting still.

ISABELLA   I sent for my sister Hennie to come and join me. I said, Hennie we'll live here forever and help the natives. You can buy two sirloins of beef for what a pound of chops costs in Edinburgh. And Hennie wrote back, the dear, that yes, she would come to Hawaii if I wished, but I said she had far better stay where she was. Hennie was suited to life in Tobermory.

MARLENE   Poor Hennie.

ISABELLA   Do you have a sister?

MARLENE   Yes in fact.

ISABELLA   Hennie was happy. She was good. I did miss its face, my own pet. But I couldn't stay in Scotland. I loathed the constant murk.

MARLENE   Ah!

(*She sees* LADY NIJO *arrive.*)

NIJO   Marlene!

MARLENE   I think a drink while we wait for the others. I need a drink anyway. What a week.

NIJO   It was always the men who used to get drunk. I'd be one of the maidens, passing the sake.

ISABELLA   I've had sake. Small hot drink. Quite fortifying after a day in the wet.

NIJO   One night my father proposed three rounds of three cups, which was normal, and then the Emperor should have said three rounds of three cups, but he said three rounds of nine cups, so you can imagine. Then the Emperor passed his sake cup to my father and said, 'Let the wild goose come to me this spring.'

MARLENE   Let the what?

NIJO   It's a literary allusion to a tenth-century epic,/His Majesty was very cultured.

ISABELLA   This is the Emperor of Japan?/I once met the Emperor of Morocco.

NIJO   In fact he was the ex-Emperor.
MARLENE   But he wasn't old?/Did you, Isabella?
NIJO   Twenty-nine.
ISABELLA   Oh it's a long story.
MARLENE   Twenty-nine's an excellent age.
NIJO   Well I was only fourteen and I knew he meant
           something but I didn't know what. He sent me an
           eight-layered gown and I sent it back. So when the
           time came I did nothing but cry. My thin gowns were
           badly ripped. But even that morning when he left/–
           he'd a green
MARLENE   Are you saying he raped you?
NIJO   robe with a scarlet lining and very heavily embroidered
           trousers, I already felt different about him. It made me
           uneasy. No, of course not, Marlene, I belonged to him,
           it was what I was brought up for from a baby. I soon
           found I was sad if he stayed away. It was depressing day
           after day not knowing when he would come. I never
           enjoyed taking other women to him.
           (*The* WAITRESS *brings the wine.*)
ISABELLA   I certainly never saw my father drunk. He was a
           clergyman. / And I didn't get married till I was fifty.
NIJO   Oh, my father was a very religious man. Just before he
           died he said to me, 'Serve His Majesty, be respectful, if
           you lose his favour enter holy orders.'
MARLENE   But he meant stay in a convent, not go wandering
           round the country.
NIJO   Priests were often vagrants, so why not a nun? You
           think I shouldn't?/I still did what my father wanted.
MARLENE   No no, I think you should. I think it was wonderful.
           (DULL GRET *arrives.*)
ISABELLA   I tried to do what my father wanted.
MARLENE   Gret, good. Nijo. Gret./I know Griselda's going to be
           late, but should we wait for Joan?/Let's get you a
           drink.
           (MARLENE *pours a drink for* GRET *while the others talk.*)
ISABELLA   Gret! (*continues to* NIJO) I tried to do what my father
           wanted. I tried to be a clergyman's daughter.
           Needlework, music, charitable schemes. I had a
           tumour removed from my spine and spent a great deal
           of time on the sofa. I studied the metaphysical poets and
           hymnology./I thought I enjoyed intellectual pursuits.
NIJO   Ah, you like poetry. I come of a line of eight

	generations of poets. Father had a poem/in the anthology.
ISABELLA	My father taught me Latin although I was a girl./But really I was
MARLENE	They didn't have Latin at my school.
ISBELLA	more suited to manual work. Cooking, washing, mending, riding horses./Better than reading books, eh Gret? A rough life in the open air. ★
NIJO	Oh but I'm sure you're very clever. ★ I can't say I enjoyed my rough life. What I enjoyed most was being the Emperor's favourite/and wearing thin silk.
ISABELLA	Did you have any horses, Gret?
GRET	Pig.
	(POPE JOAN *arrives.*)
MARLENE	Oh Joan, thank God, we can order. Do you know everyone? We were just talking about learning Latin and being clever girls. Joan was by way of an infant prodigy. Of course you were. What excited you when you were ten?
JOAN	Because angels are without matter they are not individuals. Every angel is a species.
MARLENE	There you are.
	(*They laugh. They look at menus.*)

Comment and activities

Overlapping dialogue

It is unusual for a dramatist to mark the text in the way that Churchill has in her play. The overlapping dialogue is a challenge to the timing of the actors playing the parts. Here is a further explanation of what the indications / and ★ mean in practice:

ISABELLA	This is the Emperor of Japan?/I once met the Emperor of Morocco.
NIJO	In fact he was the ex-Emperor.

Nijo's cue is 'Japan', so the second part of Isabella's speech overlaps with Nijo's line.

ISABELLA	... Cooking, washing, mending, riding horses./Better than reading books eh Gret? A rough life in the open air. ★

NIJO   Oh but I'm sure you're very clever.★ I can't say I
       enjoyed my rough life.

'Riding horses' is the cue for Nijo saying 'Oh but I'm sure ...'; 'Open
air' is the cue for 'I can't say I enjoyed ...'

▷   Read the scene through in groups, perfecting the timing and the overlap-
    ping of the dialogue. Avoid drowning one another out. The dialogue may
    be overlapping but the audience should be able to hear all of it.

Picking up cues

Churchill's instructions about overlapping dialogue helps to make a
dramatic point – the characters are all so taken up with their own
lives and self-importance that they make bad listeners and so constantly interrupt one another.

But the picking up of cues is one of the skills actors have to
develop. There is nothing more damaging to the pace of a scene than
slow picking up of cues. Of course, pauses are sometimes inserted to
make a dramatic point, but that is entirely different from pauses that
should not be there because an actor has failed to pick up a cue
quickly enough. Another point to remember is that directors often
ask actors to overlap in the delivery of dialogue when they think this
will add pace to a scene.

▷   As an exercise improvise a scene in pairs in which the entire dialogue
    consists of exchanges of a few words. The objective should be to pick up
    cues quickly without straining credibility, but, in addition, to vary the pace
    with occasional pauses. Here is an example of the kind of dialogue that
    would suit this exercise:

A   Drink?
B   Thanks.
A   Ice?
B   No, straight.
A   Hungry?
B   I've eaten.
A   Restaurant?
B   Home cooking.
    (*pause*)
A   Raining?
B   Yes.
A   Miserable.
B   Yes. (*pause*) Still, it is winter.

Acting the scene

▷ Now that you have read through the scene and practised the picking up of cues in the improvisation exercise, act out the scene. Short descriptions of the characters have been supplied above. Try to give each character a distinct personality. It might help to use one piece of costume for each to symbolise something about them (e.g. for Gret, some kind of warrior's helmet).

2.4 Checklist and further resources

The following terms and ideas have been used and discussed in this chapter. Check through the list and make sure you know the meaning of each of them.

exposition	stress
theatrical means	variation of tone
pitch	vocal delivery
pace	*coup de théâtre*

For a satire on heavy-handed exposition in cliché-ridden stage thrillers, Tom Stoppard's *The Real Inspector Hound* (1968) is very suitable.

For an example of a play opening with a narrator, look at *Aunt Dan and Lemon* (1985) by Wallace Shawn.

Further examples of work by Anton Chekhov include *The Seagull* (1896) and *Cherry Orchard* (1904).

Peter Shaffer's *Black Comedy* (1965) is an ingenious example of *coup de théâtre*.

3   The language of drama

In creating a play dramatists write down words on a page. These words will eventually be spoken by actors impersonating characters on a stage in front of an audience.

The fact that the words of the dramatist will be delivered by actors in a theatre in front of a 'live' audience creates an important distinction between the language of drama and the language of literature.

3.1 The 'voice' of the dramatist

The words a dramatist writes for the actors must be 'dramatic', i.e. they must be chosen for how much they add to the dramatic situation or as an expression of character or theme. Actors taking part in a play almost always speak 'in character'. They exchange dialogue with other actors on stage, who are playing other roles in the drama.

The illusion is usually maintained that there is no audience in the theatre listening to those words. Audiences are usually invited to think that these people on stage are 'real' and the events are actually happening. As we have already seen, however, from the extract from 'A Man for all Seasons' (1.4), dramatists sometimes break through that illusion deliberately, breaking out of the confines of character, and make the characters speak directly to the audience.

But generally the theatrical illusion is maintained. The 'voice' each character speaks with should be an individual 'voice'. The words the actor playing a particular role speaks should ring true as the individual, authentic mouthpiece of that character. If every character speaks with the same 'voice', the same point of view, even the same rhythms, then it is very likely the dramatist has merely used the characters as mouthpieces for his or her own voice. In a sense a dramatist has to have many voices, indeed as many as there are individual characters in a play.

Theatrical language

The phrases 'theatrical language' or 'theatrical terms' mean those theatrical means, other than language, by which a play text becomes a live performance in a theatre. These include lighting, stage design, movement, mime, music, costume, dance, sound effects, make-up, special theatrical effects and many kinds of technological wizardry. The term 'theatrical language' usually excludes *words* as such and is taken to mean both those techniques peculiar to the theatre and those which they share with other performing arts.

'Pure theatre'

Sometimes it appears that there is a real gap between those who believe in a form of 'pure theatre' where language is relegated to a minor role and in which the theatrical arts are paramount, and those who value language as the main weapon in the theatrical armoury. The doctrine of pure theatre acknowledges only the specifically theatrical arts and techniques e.g. dance, mime, movement and numerous theatrical effects achieved through audio-visual means, illusion, staging, costume and *coups de théâtre*. What is undoubtedly true is that words on stage have to serve the drama; they are not like the words you read in a novel. On the other hand, actors and directors have to harness all the theatrical means at their disposal in the service of the play, and words are an important element in that endeavour. It should be stressed, however, that some plays are conceived by a group of actors and a director in largely non-verbal terms and these plays clearly can be successfully produced by applying the range of theatrical skills and techniques that professional practitioners possess.

Non-verbal theatre: Jonathan Miller, *an interview*

Below is an extract from an interview given by Jonathan Miller, who is generally thought of as one of the most gifted British theatre directors. In the interview he delivers what amounts to a polemic against what he considers to be a fashionable trend towards non-verbal theatre; it is also an impassioned plea for the central import-ance of language in drama. The kind of non-verbal theatre he appears to be attacking are theatrical experiments where intelligible language is relegated to a very minor role or even where a language is invented by the actors. These are the kind of theatrical performances in which purely theatrical means such as mime, movement, dance, ritual, visual display, gesture and sounds dominate. When you are reading the extracts from the interview, consider what kind of theatre Miller is defending. What clues does he give about this in what he says?

> There's a great dogma around at the moment about non-verbal
> forms in the theatre and that somehow the use of language is

degenerate, or a corrupt piece of capitalist property: that language is the property of the Establishment and the simple, the primitive and the *folk* is really what theatre is all about, and that underneath the spoken language there is another form of communication, much richer, hotter and more communicative than anything we do in terms of words. That seems to me to be absolute rubbish. Language is the leading edge of the human personality. It's the only form of communication in which we can express the subtle discriminations that make us different from savages. I don't think that civilisation is a degeneration from savagery, and I think anything that refines and makes language more accurate is a better form of theatre. This doesn't mean I want all theatre reduced to radio; it has to be given the forms we normally do by using our hands, clothes and lights but if you remove language and only have clothes, gestures and light it's simply having a body without a skeleton. Language is the flexible skeleton of the human imagination.

Everything that human beings have done that distinguish us from animals comes from our capacity to use language. It's the duty of everyone who works in the theatre to honour language first and foremost. Ballet and mime are a naive form of art, you only suffer them on the understanding that they are abstentions from the main task, which is language. If you say you reach a larger audience without using language you might say you reach even more people by tickling them with ostrich feathers. You reach a large number of people at a crude biological level.

The thing about language is that it actually says something, it makes assertions about the world; you cannot, wagging a bamboo pole and with bizarre make-up and with a lot of groans and hums, tell anything about a scene which is not immediately there. You cannot recall the past, recall a memory, you cannot indicate anxieties about the future. The whole thing about language is that you can express subtle discriminating anxieties about the future.

Comment and activities

If you remove language and only have clothes, gestures and lights it's simply like having a body without a skeleton.

This is Miller's strongly-held view about the importance of language in theatre.

▷ Improvise a scene in any of the locations below in which someone enters and disturbs the normal routine or ambience of the place in some way:

a library	a train compartment	a launderette
a pub	a supermarket	

▷ Improvise two versions of this situation. The first version should concentrate on the spoken interchanges among the characters involved in the scene. The second version should relegate language to a minor role and be realised in terms of movement, gesture, mime, dance or any other non-verbal theatrical means you like.

▷ When you have completed these two improvisations, consider the differences between the two. How did words add something to the improvisation that non-verbal communication could not match? In which ways was the second version more or less effective because of the absence of many words? Which of the two improvisations did you prefer taking part in?

3.2 Naturalism and naturalistic language

Naturalism in the theatre attempts to portray on stage life as it really is. Naturalistic drama does not use theatrical 'tricks' or many of the theatre's conventions. In that way it is very different from the kind of non-verbal theatrical experiment that Miller is attacking in 3.1. Non-verbal theatre embraces with enthusiasm all forms of theatrical artifice; naturalism shuns them because they are artificial and not of real life. The aim of naturalistic drama is to convince the audience they are looking at an exact representation of real life on stage (for the contrast with 'realism', see 1.3).

Selectivity

But how can an exact representation of life be staged when dramatists, actors and directors are hemmed in by the limitations of the stage itself and the time an audience is willing to spend in a theatre? Obviously the dramatist has to select what he or she presents in this 'slice of life'. Incidents must be chosen that

○ are capable of being dramatised
○ can be represented on a stage
○ are of intrinsic interest to an audience
○ will make some dramatic point

Naturalistic language

Naturalistic drama demands naturalistic language i.e. the language of everyday speech. The aim of naturalistic drama is to reproduce as faithfully as possible the ordinary speech of ordinary people. Much contemporary television drama uses naturalistic language, reproducing the colloquial speech of ordinary people set against naturalistic backgrounds (e.g. in the soap operas *Coronation Street* and *East-Enders*).

'A good ear'

A naturalistic dramatist clearly needs to 'have a good ear' for ordinary speech. The dramatist must be able to recognise its rhythms and its idioms; he or she may also want to use ordinary speech to suggest a 'sub-text' that is being communicated beneath the surface meaning. Sub-text is a term used to mean what is left unsaid in exchanges between characters; these 'unspoken words' may be the substance of what is really being communicated between characters (see also 3.6). Actors and directors have to be aware of the sub-text of dialogue, if it exists.

Edward Bond, *Saved*

Edward Bond is a contemporary British playwright whose first success in the theatre, *Saved* (1965), was a naturalistic drama about extremely inarticulate people living in South London in the 1960s. Since then Bond has moved away from naturalism and written plays that are full of an austere poetry and symbolism. In *Saved*, however, he pared down the language to the barest bones because he was reproducing the ordinary, everyday speech of people who were not very fluent or able to express their feelings in terms of language.

In this extract from the play Pam enters the room where Len, a young man she is living with, is talking to an elderly man, Harry, who also shares the house in South London with them.

> PAM *comes in. She has her hair in a towel. She carries a portable radio. Someone is talking. She sits on the couch and finds a pop programme. She tunes in badly. She interrupts this from time to time to rub her hair.*
>
> LEN   (*to* HARRY) 'Ow about doin' my shirt?
>   (*He laughs.* PAM *finishes tuning. She looks round.*)
> PAM   'Oo's got my *Radio Times*? You 'ad it?
>   (HARRY *doesn't answer. She turns to* LEN.)
>   You?

LEN   (*mumbles*) Not again.

PAM   You speakin' t' me?

LEN   I'm sick t' death a yer bloody *Radio Times*.

PAM   Someone's 'ad it. (*She rubs her hair vigorously.*) I ain'
    goin' a get it no more. Not after last week. I'll cancel it.
    It's the last time I bring it in this 'ouse. I don't see why I
    'ave t' go on paying for it. Yer must think I'm made a
    money. It's never 'ere when I wan'a see it. Not once.
    It's always the same. (*She rubs her hair.*) I notice no one
    else offers t' pay for it. Always Charlie. It's 'appened
    once too often this time.

LEN   Every bloody week the same!

PAM   (*to* HARRY) Sure yer ain' got it?

HARRY   I bought this shirt over eight years ago.

PAM   That cost me every week. You reckon that up over a
    year. Yer must think I was born yesterday.
    (*Pause. She rubs her hair.*)
    Wasn't 'ere last week. Never 'ere. Got legs.
    (*She goes to the door and shouts.*)
    Mum! She 'eard all right.
    (*She goes back to the couch and sits. She rubs her hair.*)
    Someone's got it. I shouldn't think the people next door
    come in an' took it. Everyone 'as the benefit a it 'cept
    me. It's always the same. I'll know what t' do in future.
    Two can play at that game. I ain' blinkin' daft. (*She rubs
    her hair.*) I never begrudge no one borrowin' it, but
    yer'd think they'd have enough manners t' put it back.
    (*Pause. She rubs her hair.*)
    Juss walk all over yer. Well it ain' goin' a 'appen again.
    They treat you like a door mat. All take and no give.
    Touch somethin' a their'n an' they go through the
    bloody ceilin'. It's bin the same ever since –

LEN   I tol' yer t' keep it in yer room!

PAM   Now yer got a lock things up in yer own 'ouse.

LEN   Why should we put up with this week after week juss
    because yer too –

PAM   Yer know what yer can do.

LEN   Thass yer answer t' everythin'.

PAM   Got a better one?

HARRY   They was a pair first off. Set me back a quid each. Up
    the market. One's gone 'ome, went at the cuffs. Worth
    a quid.

LEN   Chriss.

Comment and activities

Preparing to perform a scene

As pointed out before (see 1.3), actors usually give themselves clear objectives in each scene they are involved in. They discuss with the director and the other actors how their part in the scene should be interpreted, how their lines should be delivered, what moves, if any, they should make, how they should react to what the others on stage say and do, and how they can contribute to the overall pacing of the scene.

Rehearsal notes

It is normal practice for actors rehearsing a scene to make brief notes on their script to remind them of moves, matters of interpretation, vocal delivery, stress etc.

The actress playing Pam in this scene could have these notes written into her script:

PAM   *comes in. She has her hair in a towel. She carries a portable radio.*

Someone is talking. She sits on the couch and finds a pop programme. She With signs of irritation *tunes in badly. She interrupts this from time to time to rub her hair.* vigorously

LEN   (*to* HARRY) 'Ow about doin' my shirt?

(*He laughs.* PAM *finishes tuning. She looks round.*)

PAM   'Oo's got my *Radio Times?* You'ad it?
aggressively

(HARRY *doesn't answer. She turns to* LEN.)

You?

LEN   (*mumbles*) Not again.

PAM   You speakin' t' me?   Sarcastically

LEN   I'm sick t' death a yer bloody *Radio Times*.

PAM   Someone's 'ad it. (*She rubs her hair vigorously.*) I ain' goin' a

get it no more. Not after last week. I'll cancel it. It's the

as a threat

last time I bring it in this 'ouse. I don't see why I 'ave t' go

almost speaking

on paying for it. Yer must think I'm made a money. It's

to herself

never 'ere when I wan'a see it. Not once. It's always the

same. (*She rubs her hair.*) I notice no one else offers t' pay

with even more vigour

for it. Always Charlie. It's 'appened once too often this

you treat me   *emphatic*

time.   *like dirt*

When actors have to deliver a speech of any length they have to consider ways of varying their delivery – the emphasis they give different words, the pitch of their voice, the tone and the pace they use. If they say every line of a speech in more or less the same way, then the audience will probably switch off and stop listening. In real life most people instinctively vary the pitch, tone and pace of their speech, especially when they are trying to communicate something they care about, as Pam is doing in this scene. The actor playing Pam in this scene must start from her understanding of the feelings Pam is expressing through her words, and then find ways of varying the manner of her delivery.

Listening and responding to the other actors

Actors must really listen to the other actors on the stage. Their responses must make it appear as though they are hearing what is being said to them for the first time. Their lines must come out as though they are saying them for the very first time. They must also avoid picking up one another's intonations or vocal qualities.

Directing and directors' notes

In rehearsal the director has to be the sounding-board for the actors. The director should be able to advise the actors about vocal delivery, pitch, pace and interpretation. The director should be alive to the 'sub-text' – or underlying, unspoken meaning – of the scene. It is often what the characters are not saying to one another that is the most important element in the scene. A skilful director should be able to make the sub-text clear to an audience, or at least suggest it to them. In rehearsal a director will often react spontaneously to what is happening among the actors and accept suggestions they make about the playing of a scene. The director will make suggestions of his or her own, on the spur of the moment. But it is also necessary for the director to prepare for rehearsing a scene by noting beforehand opportunities for things like variation, change of pace or mood, and clarifying the sub-text of a scene.

Here are the kind of notes a director might make about a section of the scene above:

> LEN   Every bloody week the same!
>   *muted*
>
> PAM   (*to* HARRY) Sure yer ain' got it?
>   *attacking Len for his neglect*
>
> HARRY I bought this shirt over eight years ago.
>
> PAM   That cost me every week. You reckon that over a year.
>   *You don't appreciate me*
>   Yer must think I was born yesterday.
>   *You treat me like a fool*
>   (*Pause. She rubs her hair.*)

Within that short scene the director is guiding the actors towards varying the delivery of the lines. Pauses and stresses are used to underline the dramatic situation and how each character is reacting to it.

Here are some notes a director might make about aims concerning the sub-text of this scene:

Pam : jealous of the bond between Len and Harry; feels neglected; 'Radio Times' just a pretext to express her sense of frustration and neglect.

Len : resents her presence and her attack; defensive.

Harry: his defence is to draw in on himself; he acts as though Pam is not there; ignores tension.

Clarifying the sub-text will underline the dramatic tension for the audience; it will make them think about what the characters are *really* saying to one another.

Acting the scene

▷   Working in groups with one person taking the role of the director, rehearse this scene for performance, taking into account the advice about pace and delivery and the bringing out of the sub-text. As you rehearse discuss the language and how it can be interpreted to bring out the full dramatic potential of the scene. Both actors and directors should make brief notes on the scene. Remember also that this is an example of naturalistic drama; the style of acting and direction should recognise that.

▷   The play is set in the 1960s, but there is little reason why the play could not be performed in a contemporary setting. The social background is deprived and working-class; the setting is an inner-city environment. If you were designing the set and/or the costumes for a production set in the present, what kind of design would you use to underline the bleak view of the characters' existence which the playwright is presenting? If possible, do a detailed illustration of the set and the furniture you would use and/or the clothes you would have the three characters wear.

3.3   The language of high comedy

'High comedy' is a term usually applied to comic plays that deal, often satirically, with the social customs and mores of the upper classes. High comedy had one of its most fertile periods after the Restoration, during Charles II's reign (1660-85). Cromwell and the Puritans had closed the theatres in 1642, because they were thought to be a danger to public morality, but eighteen years later the Restoration brought a new licence to the public stage.

Playwrights such as Congreve, Wycherley, Otway, Farquhar, Vanburgh, Etherege and Behn used this new freedom to people the stages with the fops, the society lords and ladies, the 'nouveau riche' of the upper bourgeoisie, the erring husbands and wives, the mistresses and whores, the rakes and young-men-on-the-make who no doubt were prominent in real-life London society.

Themes

These Restoration plays are concerned with the antics of the upper classes in their quest for money, property, social status, sex in the form of illicit alliances, reputation; and their fear of poverty, exclusion from this privileged society and fear of being 'cuckolded' (a cuckold was a husband whose wife was committing adultery) or exposed as a fornicator. There is also at least one character in most Restoration plays who is on the fringe of this affluent society and who desperately wants to gain entry through making a 'good' marriage. Marriage and property are inextricably intertwined in this society; married love and romantic or sexual love are seen as quite different from one another. The lower classes appear only as servants.

The social life portrayed in the plays has a surface glitter, a flamboyant style, an elegance of manner, dress and language that only faintly mask the anxieties and amorality that lies at the heart of society.

The language of Restoration comedy

The language used by Edward Bond in *Saved* (3.2) imitated everyday speech. It is as close as is possible to the way a certain class of people living in a certain environment at a certain time spoke. The society the late seventeenth-century dramatists wrote about could scarcely be more different. The spare vernacular of Bond's characters is replaced with the elaborate and sometimes flowery speech of people moving in a leisurely, wealthy, competitive and superficially assured, upper-class society. How close the words used by these dramatists in their plays are to the actual speech of this class in their time is difficult for us to assess, but we must assume it bears a close resemblance.

The language poses challenges to actors, directors and audiences. It must be delivered in an intelligible way and appear to come naturally out of the mouths of actors playing seventeenth-century people.

William Wycherley, *The Country Wife*

William Wycherley was one of the most prominent of the Restoration dramatists. *The Country Wife* (1675) is probably his most famous play, and is a satire on the social and moral hypocrisy of the upper-class society of the time. Wycherley's main purpose, apart from entertaining his audience, is to expose the superficial moral poses of his characters and the corruption beneath the thin layer of moralising that many of them indulge in. Alongside the moral protestation there is a good deal of sexual innuendo.

In this extract from *The Country Wife,* three society ladies, Lady Fidget, Mrs Dainty Fidget and Mrs Squeamish, have visited Pinchwife's house to take his young wife – the 'country wife' of the title – to the theatre. Pinchwife is desperate to keep his wife locked up, away from the temptations of society. He makes the excuse that his wife has the smallpox and leaves the women alone together.

MRS SQUEAMISH	Here's an example of jealousy!
LADY FIDGET	Indeed, as the world goes. I wonder there are no more jealous, since wives are so neglected.
MRS DAINTY	Pshaw! as the world goes, to what end should they be jealous?
LADY FIDGET	Foh! 'tis a nasty world.
MRS SQUEAMISH	That men of parts, great acquaintance, and quality, should take up with and spend themselves and fortunes in keeping little playhouse creatures, foh!
LADY FIDGET	Nay, that women of understanding, great acquaintance, and good quality, should fall a-keeping too of little creatures, foh!
MRS SQUEAMISH	Why, 'tis the men of quality's fault; they never visit women of honour and reputation as they

	used to do; and have not so much as common civility for ladies of our rank, but use us with the same indifferency and ill-breeding as if we were all married to 'em.
LADY FIDGET	She says true; 'tis an arrant shame women of quality should be so slighted; methinks birth – birth should go for something; I have known men admired, courted, and followed for their titles only.
MRS SQUEAMISH	Ay, one would think men of honour should not love, no more than marry, out of their own rank.
MRS DAINTY	Fy, fy, upon 'em! they are come to think cross breeding for themselves best, as well as for their dogs and horses.
LADY FIDGET	They are dogs and horses for't.
MRS SQUEAMISH	One would think, if not for love, for vanity a little.
MRS DAINTY	Nay, they do satisfy their vanity upon us sometimes; and are kind to us in their report, tell all the world they lie with us.
LADY FIDGET	Damned rascals, that we should be only wronged by 'em! To report a man has had a person, when he has not had a person, is the greatest wrong in the whole world that can be done to a person.
MRS SQUEAMISH	Well, 'tis an arrant shame noble persons should be so wronged and neglected.
LADY FIDGET	But still 'tis an arranter shame for a noble person to neglect her own honour, and defame her own noble person with little inconsiderable fellows, foh!
MRS DAINTY	I suppose the crime against our honour is the same with a man of quality as with another.
LADY FIDGET	How! no, sure, the man of quality is likest one's husband, and therefore the fault should be the less.
MRS DAINTY	But then the pleasure should be the less.
LADY FIDGET	Fy, fy, fy, for shame, sister! whither shall we ramble? Be continent in your discourse, or I shall hate you.

Comment and activities

Playing high comedy, and especially high comedy written around three hundred years ago, demands a lot from actors and directors. There is firstly the challenge the language poses. Many of the words, the idioms, the rhythms and sentence constructions are very different to contemporary usage so actors have to make their delivery seem natural and make it intelligible to modern audiences. Their delivery of the words must do justice to the elegance and wit of the language.

Style

The other problem for actors and directors in producing Restoration comedy is the matter of 'style'. Acting style should emerge naturally from the dramatic situations, setting, language and the overall feel of a play. Too often, however, even professional actors and directors settle for 'reach-me-down' acting styles taken from the 'coarse acting' shelves where such easy solutions are stored. 'Ah, this week it's Restoration comedy so we need plenty of exaggerated playing, crude comic business, swooping voices, lots of flounces and epigrams delivered as though they are one-liners from a stand-up comedian.' At its worst this adoption of a ready-made style results in a shallow, superficial and supposedly audience-pleasing attempt to get easy laughs.

More skilful and serious actors and directors, however, will aim for something more substantial and sensitive and obviously the manner in which they handle the language of Restoration comedy will be crucial to this.

The rhythms of the language

Actors playing in Restoration comedy have to give a good deal of thought to the rhythms and structures of the language. Sentences, for example, tend to be longer and more formal in structure than in contemporary drama. A professional actor or serious amateur would study his or her speeches before rehearsal and discuss with the director how they should be delivered. Below are some notes on how one speech by Mrs Squeamish from the extract could be delivered. Where 'rising' and 'falling' are indicated below, these terms refer to intonation (i.e. the upwards and downwards pitch of the voice in the speaking of a sentence).

MRS SQUEAMISH   Why, 'tis the men of quality's fault; they
rising, emphatic tone

never visit women of honour and reputation
stress   stress

as they used to do; and have not so much as
falling (pause)   caustic

common civility for ladies of our rank, but
stress   stress

use us with the same indifferency and ill-
stress   downwards

breeding as if we were all married to 'em.
rising →

▷   Of course, there is no one way of delivering the above speech; individual
     actors would have their own approach to it. Try delivering the speech
     according to the advice given above. The tone of the speech should be
     self-righteous, suggesting hypocrisy on the part of the character.

▷   Now consider the two speeches below. Decide how they should be
     phrased, what kind of varied intonation could be used and what tone they
     should be delivered in. Make brief notes on the speeches in the same way
     as has been done above.

MRS DAINTY   Nay, they do satisfy their vanity upon us
              sometimes; and are kind to us in their report,
              tell all the world they lie with us.
LADY FIDGET   Damned rascals, that we should only be
              wronged by 'em! To report a man has had a
              person, when he has not had a person, is the
              greatest wrong in the whole world that can be
              done to a person.

Acting the scene

▷   Once you have worked on individual speeches, rehearse the whole scene in
     groups with one person acting as director. Decide what you want to convey to an
     audience about the characters. Are they being hypocritical? Is the dramatist's
     intention to expose their real inclinations behind their veneer of moral respec-
     tability? If so, then that should come out in the performance. As an aid to your

performance, choose one small item of costume (a hat or a fan, perhaps) which will 'stand in' for the type of elaborate dress that seventeenth-century society women would have worn.

3.4 Seventeenth-century verse drama

The greatest flowering of verse drama (i.e. drama written largely in verse) occurred in the last few decades of the sixteenth and first few decades of the seventeenth century. It was then that Shakespeare, Marlowe, Jonson, Ford, Webster, Beaumont and Fletcher, Heywood, Middleton and many others were writing plays for the entertainment and enlightenment of Elizabethan and Jacobean audiences. People do not speak in verse in real life, although the characteristics we associate with poetry – rhythm, imagery, repetition, assonance and alliteration – are all present in everyday speech. Verse drama, then, is not naturalistic; Elizabethans and Jacobeans did not go round exchanging conversation in iambic pentameter.

Themes

Most of the dramatists of this period dealt with heroic themes: their characters were usually persons of note or great worth. There were few plays written about ordinary people, although the emerging bourgeoisie were beginning to be portrayed on stage. Heroic themes and characters found their natural expression in a heightening of language, with thoughts and emotions condensed into images that illuminate and set off ripples of meaning, and hint at universal truths. Dramatists felt the need to use verse to match the intensity of the themes and the importance of their characters.

Dramatic verse

However, in a play, dramatic verse has to perform several functions. It must be dramatic – it must carry the action forward; it cannot only be reflective; it can very rarely be merely decorative. Within the dramatic verse the dramatist has to find separate 'voices' for each of his characters. Dramatic verse often has to be expository: it has to explain the dramatic situation to the audience – and it is true to say that this is sometimes rather clumsily done in the early verse plays of this period. It is interesting to note that prose is often used in particular scenes of verse plays: when characters from the lower classes appear, as servants or figures of fun, acting as comic relief amidst an intense tragedy, they are given prose to speak.

John Webster, *The Duchess of Malfi*

John Webster was one of the leading Jacobean dramatists. His plays
are a sombre picture of Jacobean society; their themes are the corrupt-
ibility and cruelty of human nature. These themes find their expression in verse that is laden with images of death and decay.

The final scene from the production of *The Duchess of Malfi* at the National
Theatre in 1985. As is usual with Jacobean and Elizabethan tragedies, the stage at
the end of the play is littered with dead bodies.

The Duchess of Malfi (1614) is a special type of tragedy called a
'revenge tragedy', a popular form with the audiences of the day. In
revenge tragedies, the hero is set the task of revenging an injustice, a
task which he is honour-bound to complete, but which inevitably
leads to his destruction. (We will go into more detail about revenge
tragedy in 5.2 when we look at an extract from Shakespeare's *Hamlet*,
certainly the most famous of all the revenge tragedies.) The corruption portrayed in Webster's play makes the corrupt characters in
Wycherley's *The Country Wife* seem almost petty. This is a society
where no quarter is given, where treachery abounds and anything
goes in an amoral and arbitrary world. In this extract from the play,
Ferdinand, the Duke of Calabria, visits his sister, the Duchess of
Malfi, whom he has imprisoned for having married secretly, and
borne children to, the master of her household. Ferdinand is intent
on extracting the utmost revenge for what he considers to be her
treachery. Bosola is a ruthless mercenary in the pay of Ferdinand.

    Enter DUCHESS
        BOSOLA   All comfort to your grace.
        DUCHESS   I will have none.
                      Pray thee, why dost thou wrap thy poisoned pills
                      In gold and sugar?

BOSOLA   Your elder brother, the Lord Ferdinand
              Is come to visit you, and sends you word,
              'Cause once he rashly made a solemn vow
              Never to see you more, he comes i' the night;
              And prays you gently neither torch nor taper
              Shine in your chamber: he will kiss your hand,
              And reconcile himself; but for this vow
              He dares not see you.
DUCHESS   At his pleasure –
              Take hence the lights – He's come.
              (*enter* FERDINAND)
FERDINAND   Where are you?
DUCHESS   Here, sir.
FERDINAND   This darkness suits you well.
DUCHESS   I would ask you pardon.
FERDINAND   You have it;
              For I account it the honourabl'st revenge,
              Where I may kill, to pardon – Where are your
                  cubs?
DUCHESS   Whom?
FERDINAND   Call them your children;
              For though our national law distinguish bastards
              From true legitimate issue, compassionate nature
              Makes them all equal.
DUCHESS   Do you visit me for this?
              You violate a sacrament o' the church
              Shall make you howl in hell for 't.
FERDINAND   It had been well
              Could you have lived thus always; for, indeed,
              You were too much i' the light: but no more –
              I come to seal my peace with you. Here's a hand.
              (*gives her a dead man's hand*)
              To which you have vowed much love; the ring
                  upon 't
              You gave.
DUCHESS   I affectionately kiss it.
FERDINAND   Pray, do, and bury the print of it in your heart.
              I will leave this ring with you for a love token;
              And the hand as sure as the ring; and do not doubt
              But you shall have the heart too: when you need a
                  friend,
              Send it to him that owned it; you shall see
              Whether he can aid you.

DUCHESS   You are very cold:
           I fear you are not well after your travel –
           Ha! Lights! – oh horrible!
FERDINAND Let her have lights enough! (*exit*)
DUCHESS   What witchcraft does he practise that he hath left
           A dead man's hand here?
           (*Here is discovered, behind a traverse the artificial figures
           of* ANTONIO *and his children, appearing as if they were
           dead.*)
BOSOLA   Look you, here's the piece from which it was ta'en.
           He doth present you this sad spectacle,
           That, now you know directly they are dead,
           Hereafter you may wisely cease to grieve
           From that which cannot be recovered.
DUCHESS   There is not between heaven and earth one wish
           I stay for after this: it wastes me more
           Than were't my picture, fashioned out of wax,
           Stuck with a magical needle, and then buried
           In some foul dunghill; and yond's an excellent
              property
           For a tyrant. Which I would account mercy.
BOSOLA   What's that?
DUCHESS   If they would bind me to that lifeless trunk,
           And let me freeze to death.
BOSOLA   Come you must live.
DUCHESS   That's the greatest torture souls feel in hell,
           In hell, that they must live, and cannot die.
           Portia, I'll new kindle thy coals again,
           And revive that rare and almost dead example
           Of a loving wife.
BOSOLA   Oh, fie! Despair? Remember
           You are a Christian.
DUCHESS   The church enjoins fasting:
           I'll starve myself to death.
BOSOLA   Leave this vain sorrow.
           Things being at the worst begin to mend: the bee
           When he hath shot his sting into your hand,
           May then play with your eyelid.
DUCHESS   Good comfortable fellow,
           Persuade a wretch that's broke upon the wheel
           To have all his bones new set; entreat him live
           To be executed again. Who must dispatch me?
           I account this world a tedious theatre,
           For I do play a part in 't 'gainst my will.

BOSOLA	Come, be of comfort; I will save your life.
DUCHESS	Indeed, I have not leisure to tend
	So small a business.
BOSOLA	Now, by my life, I pity you.
DUCHESS	Thou are a fool, then,
	To waste thy pity on a thing so wretched
	As cannot pity itself. I am full of daggers.
	Puff, let me blow these vipers from me.
	(*enter* SERVANT)
	What are you?
SERVANT	One that wishes you long life.
DUCHESS	I would thou wert hanged for the horrible curse
	Thou hast given me: I shall shortly grow one
	Of the miracles of pity. I'll go pray;
	No, I'll go curse.
BOSOLA	Oh, fie!

Comment and activities

In this scene a brother offers his sister in a darkened room a severed hand to be kissed and arranges for waxwork effigies of her husband and children to be displayed to her to look as though they are corpses. His intention is to torture his sister and drive her insane. Described like this, we could be talking about a ghoulish scene from a contemporary horror film. Undoubtedly Jacobean audiences liked scenes of horror and torture, blood and gore. Sometimes, as in this scene, the element of horror teeters on the edge of being comic; it is only really the intensity of Webster's poetic vision that raises the drama to the level of heroic tragedy.

An analysis of a speech by the Duchess

The Duchess reacts to the horror with stoic eloquence:

DUCHESS	There is not between heaven and earth one wish
	I stay for after this; it wastes me more
	Than were't my picture, fashioned out of wax,
	Stuck with a magical needle, and then buried
	In some foul dunghill; and yond's an excellent
	property
	For a tyrant which I would account mercy.
BOSOLA	What's that?
DUCHESS	If they could bind me to that lifeless trunk
	And let me freeze to death.

Actors speaking dramatic verse have to be sensitive to the rhythms
and imagery. They must not declaim the verse but interpret it according to the emotional truth of the words. The rhythms of the verse will
tell them a lot. Obviously the dramatic situation is an important
factor. In this scene, having witnessed such scenes, the Duchess
could react with hysterical outpourings and the speech above could
be delivered in that manner. But not if the rhythms of the verse are
listened to.
Say these two lines aloud to yourself:

> There is not between heaven and earth one wish
> I stay for after this;

There is a note of flat resignation in this speech, which is expressed in
monosyllabic words. The rhythms direct the actor to speak the verse
in a restrained manner; I think it would be quite wrong to deliver
them in an emotional or hysterical manner.

Run-on and end-stop lines

When speaking dramatic verse you should follow the sense and the
flow of the verse. Sometimes lines flow into one another without
pause; these lines are called run-on lines, or examples of 'enjambement.' Other lines have a pause at the end; (either a slight pause,
usually marked with a comma, or a more definite break marked by
full stop or a semi-colon). These lines are referred to as end-stop lines.

▷   Look at the analysis of a speech by the Duchess below; (ES) means an
     end-stop line, ⟩ means a run-on line.

     DUCHESS   Good comfortable fellow, (ES)
               Persuade a wretch that's broke upon the wheel ⟩
               To have all his bones new set; entreat him live ⟩
               To be executed again. Who must dispatch me? (ES)
               I account this world a tedious theatre, (ES)
               For I do play a part in 't 'gainst my will. (ES)

Of these six lines, four are end-stop lines and two are run-on lines.
Notice also how two of the lines have definite pauses in mid-line,
marked by a semi-colon and a full stop respectively.
   The actor thinking about how to deliver this speech must start from
how she and the director interpret the emotional state of the character in the dramatic situation she finds herself in, but she must also
consider the technical features of the verse which help to underline
the emotions.

▷   Discuss how any of the other speeches of the Duchess in this scene would be spoken, remembering the dramatic situation and her reaction to the gruesome spectacle she has witnessed. Work in pairs, with a director, concentrating on speaking the verse with the appropriate emotion and interpretation.

▷   A director directing a scene of any length should usually be looking for opportunities to bring out contrasts between characters so that, through the contrast, each becomes more defined. If you were directing the actors in this scene what advice would you give them about vocal delivery, manner, gesture and movement to bring out the contrast between Bosola and the Duchess in the first section of the scene, Ferdinand and the Duchess in the middle section and Bosola and the Duchess in the last section?

▷   Webster's vision of a corrupt and cruel world finds expression in imagery of torture and malevolence. Analyse the verse, tracing the use of images of this kind, and say how you might bring these out in performance.

Acting the scene

▷   The scene is meant to take place in the dark, but obviously the stage cannot be in complete darkness or the audience would get restless. Lighting used for dramatic purposes can add considerably to the impact of this scene. Divide the scene into three main sections – the dialogue between Bosola and the Duchess; the Duchess and Ferdinand; and the revelation of the waxworks. What lighting would you use that would most effectively underline the drama in these three sections?

▷   Now rehearse the whole scene in groups with one person acting as director.

3.5   The poetry of ordinary speech

J. M. Synge, *The Playboy of the Western World*

J. M. Synge (1871–1909) was an Irish dramatist who wrote his prose plays in the first decade of this century. The language of his plays, he claimed, was taken straight from the mouths of ordinary Irish country people. Here is an extract from the preface Synge wrote for the publication of his most famous play *The Playboy of the Western World* (1907).

It is probable that when the Elizabethan dramatist took his ink-horn and sat down to his work he used many phrases that he had just heard, as he sat at dinner, from his mother or his children. In Ireland those of us who know the people have the same privilege. When I was writing 'The Shadow of the Glen' some years ago, I got more aid than any learning could have given me from a chink in the floor of the old Wicklow house where I was staying, that let me hear what was being said by the servant girls in the kitchen. This matter, I think, is of importance, for in countries where the imagination of the people, and the language they use, is rich and living, it is possible for a writer to be rich and copious in his words, and at the same time to give the reality, which is the root of all poetry, in a comprehensive and natural form.

In the modern literature of towns, however, richness is found only in sonnets, or prose poems, or in one or two elaborate books that are far away from the profound and common interests of life. On the stage one must have reality and one must have joy; and that is why the modern intellectual drama has failed, and the people have grown sick of the false joy of the musical comedy, that has been given them in place of the rich joy found only in what is superb and wild in reality. In a good play every speech should be as fully flavoured as a nut or apple, and such speeches cannot be written by anyone who works among people who have shut their lips on poetry. In Ireland for a few years more, we have a popular imagination that is fiery, and magnificent, and tender; and so those of us who wish to write start with a chance that is not given to writers in places where the spring-time of the local life has been forgotten, and the harvest is a memory only, and the straw has been turned into bricks.

Synge claims that the language of his plays comes more or less straight from the mouths of the country people of Ireland; townspeople have largely lost their contact with poetic speech; and dramatists such as Ibsen reflect this in the 'pallid prose' they employ in their plays. The other important claim Synge makes in his preface is that 'reality' is 'the root of all poetry' and every speech in a play must be as fully flavoured 'as a nut or apple'.

Whether these are largely romantic assertions on the part of Synge or not you may be able to judge in part by this extract from *The Playboy of the Western World*. In the first act of the play, Christy Mahon, a fugitive, has stumbled into the rough, countryside public house run by Michael James and his daughter, Pegeen. Christy confesses to his astonished audience that he has killed his own father.

Word of this spreads round the district and the Widow Quin, a woman of about thirty, comes to the shebeen, where Christy and Pegeen have been left alone together, to see this 'wonder'.

PEGEEN	(*pointing to* CHRISTY) Look now is he roaring, and he stretched out drowsy with his supper and his mug of milk. Walk down and tell that to Father Reilly and the Shaneen Keogh.
WIDOW QUIN	(*coming forward*) I'll not see them again, for I've their word to lead that lad forward for to lodge with me.
PEGEEN	(*in blank amazement*) This night is it?
WIDOW QUIN	(*going over*) This night. 'It isn't fitting,' says the priesteen, 'to have his likeness lodging with an orphaned girl.' (to CHRISTY) God save you, mister!
CHRISTY	(*shyly*) God save you kindly!
WIDOW QUIN	(*looking at him with half-amused curiosity*) Well, aren't you a little smiling fellow? It should have been great and bitter torments did rouse your spirits to a deed of blood.
CHRISTY	(*doubtfully*) It should, maybe.
WIDOW QUIN	It's more than 'maybe' I'm saying, and it'd soften my heart to see you sitting so simple with your cup and cake, and you fitter to be saying your catechism than slaying your da.
PEGEEN	(*at counter, washing glasses*) There's talking when any'd see he's fit to be holding his head high with the wonders of the world. Walk on from this, for I'll not have him tormented, and he destroyed travelling since Tuesday was a week.
WIDOW QUIN	(*peaceably*) We'll be walking surely when his supper's done, and you'll find we're great company, young fellow, when it's of the like of you and me you'd hear the penny poets singing in an August Fair.
CHRISTY	(*innocently*) Did you kill your father?
PEGEEN	(*contemptuously*) She did not. She hit himself with a worn pick, and the rusted poison did corrode his blood the way he never overed it, and died after. That was a sneaky kind of murder did win small glory with the boys itself. (*She crosses to* CHRISTY's *left.*)

WIDOW QUIN	(*with good-humour*) If it didn't, maybe all knows a widow woman has buried her children and destroyed her man is a wiser comrade for a young lad than a girl, the like of you, who'd go helter-skeltering after any man would let you a wink upon the road.
PEGEEN	(*breaking out into wild rage*) And you'll say that, Widow Quin, and you gasping with the rage you had racing the hill beyond to look on his face.
WIDOW QUIN	(*laughing derisively*) Me, is it? Well, Father Reilly has cuteness to divide you now. (*She pulls* CHRISTY *up.*) There's great temptation in a man did slay his da, and we'd best be going, young fellow; so rise up and come with me.
PEGEEN	(*seizing his arm*) He'll not stir. He's pot-boy in this place, and I'll not have him stolen off and kidnapped while himself's abroad.
WIDOW QUIN	It'd be a crazy pot-boy'd lodge him in the shebeen where he works by day, so you'd have a right to come on, young fellow, till you see my little houseen, a perch off on the rising hill.
PEGEEN	Wait till morning, Christy Mahon. Wait till you lay eyes on her leaky thatch is growing more pasture for her buck goat than her square of fields, and she without a tramp itself to keep in order her place at all.
WIDOW QUIN	When you see me contriving in my little gardens, Christy Mahon, you'll swear the Lord God formed me to be living lone, and that there isn't my match in Mayo for thatching, or mowing, or shearing a sheep.
PEGEEN	(*with noisy scorn*) It's true the Lord God formed you to contrive indeed. Doesn't the world know you reared a black ram at your own breast, so that the Lord Bishop of Connaught felt the elements of a Christian, and he eating it after in a kidney stew? Doesn't the world know you've been seen shaving the foxy skipper from France for a threepenny-bit and a sop of grass tobacco would wring the liver from a mountain goat you'd meet leaping the hills?
WIDOW QUIN	(*with amusement*) Do you hear her now, young

fellow? Do you hear the way she'll be rating at
your own self when a week is by?

PEGEEN   (*to* CHRISTY) Don't heed her. Tell her to go on into
her pigsty and not plague us here.

WIDOW QUIN   I'm going; but he'll come with me.

PEGEEN   (*shaking him*) Are you dumb, young fellow?

Comment and activities

Synge's language

▷   Synge says there is poetry in the speech of ordinary people in the Irish
countryside. Consider what is 'poetic' about these extracts from the
scene:

PEGEEN   Wait till morning, Christy Mahon. Wait till you
lay eyes on her leaky thatch that is growing more
pasture for her buck goat than her square of fields,
and she without a tramp itself to keep in order her
place at all.

WIDOW QUIN   When you see me contriving in my little gardens,
Christy Mahon, you'll swear the Lord God formed
me to be living lone, and there isn't my match in
Mayo for thatching, or mowing, or shearing a
sheep.

Synge states that reality is at the root of all poetry. This dramatic verse
is full of 'real' details, such as, 'leaky thatch', 'buck goat', and 'contriving in my own little gardens'.

The other essential element the language of plays should have is
'joy'. It is certainly true there is an ebullience about this language and
a delight in the sounds of words, a lilt to the rhythms of the prose. But
was this poetry, this 'joy', really there in the everyday speech of the
Irish peasantry at the turn of the century, or has Synge selected only
what is colourful and folksy for the entertainment of his audiences?
Does it matter if Synge has been selective? All dramatists have to be
selective; we have already established that in (2.1). But if the selec-
tivity tends to include only language that is chosen for its aural
impact, for its lilt and its poetic aspects, is there a danger that the
characters and the drama as a whole become stereotyped and roman-
ticised? Perhaps only native-born Irish actors can do full justice to the
poetic rhythms and sounds of Synge's language. However, when you
are speaking this dialogue, you can sense the lilt of the language, you
can allow the rhythms of the words to carry you along with it.

Acting the scene

▷   Act the scene in groups, again with one person taking on the director's role. Decide what kind of delivery the dialogue demands, how to vary the pace of the scene and how movement and gesture can add to the liveliness of the drama.

3.6   The space between words

Sub-text: Harold Pinter, *extract from a speech*

We have already used and examined the word sub-text (see 3.2). Sub-text is a term often associated with the plays of Harold Pinter. Pinter is a contemporary playwright who has created a style of writing for the theatre that is often referred to as 'Pinterish'. As a dramatist he admits to not being interested in dealing with social or political issues. His characters are supplied with little or no biographical detail; they just 'are'. The relationship of the characters to one another is often hazily sketched in, and the themes of his plays are not very specific or clear. When asked to talk about his work Pinter usually shrugs and says something like, 'The plays speak for themselves. I have no interest in analysing them. They mean what you want them to mean.' This sparseness of theme, characterisation and action is extended to the language Pinter uses. The general estimate of Pinter's dialogue is that it 'imitates' ordinary speech, but because of its subtle rhythms, repetitions and verbal resonances it goes well beyond naturalism to a kind of bleak poetry. Pinter is reticent about his own work, but below is an extract from a speech he gave at a drama festival in which he voiced his distrust of words.

> So often, below the word spoken, is the thing known and unspoken. My characters tell me so much and no more, with reference to their experience, their aspirations, their motives, their history. Between my lack of biographical data about them and the ambiguity of what they say lies a territory which is not only worthy of exploration but which it is compulsory to explore. You and I, the characters which grow on a page, most of the time we're inexpressive, giving little away, unreliable, elusive, evasive, obstructive, unwilling, but it's out of these attributes that a language arises. A language, I repeat, where under what is said, another thing is being said.
>
>   There are two silences. One when no word is spoken. The other when perhaps a torrent of language is being employed. This speech is speaking of a language locked beneath it. That is its

continual reference. The speech we hear is an indication of that which we don't hear. It is a necessary avoidance, a violent, sly, anguished or mocking smoke screen which keeps the other in its place. When true silence falls we are still left with echo but are nearer nakedness. One way of looking at speech is to say that it is a constant stratagem to cover nakedness.

We have heard many times that tired, grimy phrase 'failure of communication'. . . and this phrase has been fixed to my work quite consistently. I believe the contrary. I think we communicate only too well, in our silence, in what is unsaid, and that what takes place is a continual evasion, desperate rearguard attempts to keep ourselves to ourselves. Communication is too alarming. To enter into someone's life is too frightening. To disclose to others the poverty within us is too fearsome a possibility.

Comment and activities

We are confronted by a huge weight of words, day in, day out. The various media bombard us with words – in newspapers, on radio and television, through advertising and magazines. We are constantly being persuaded, encouraged and got at. Through the seemingly endless repetition of these phrases, slogans, orders, advice and head-lines, do the words eventually become fairly meaningless?

▷   As an exercise collect together slogans, headlines, well-known sayings and clichés of the kind you hear on television and radio, read in news-papers and magazines and overhear in everyday conversation. Arrange them in any order you like and in pairs or groups repeat them again and again to make the dramatic point of how meaningless language becomes when the same words are constantly repeated.

Pauses in speech

In Pinter's plays, as the author himself has indicated above, silences, or 'the space between words' are very important. Very often what the characters are not saying is more important than what they are saying. Words are used usually not as expression of self, but as a diguise of self.

Harold Pinter, *The Caretaker*

Below is an extract from Pinter's play *The Caretaker* (1960). Aston lives in rather a derelict house in the East End of London; he has met Davies, an elderly tramp in a nearby cafe. Davies has just been sacked from his cafe job and Aston brings him back to the house.

ASTON *stands upright, takes out his tobacco and begins to roll a cigarette. He goes to his bed and sits.*

ASTON   How are you off for money?
DAVIES Oh well . . . now, mister, if you want the truth . . . I'm a
        bit short.
        (ASTON *takes some coins from his pocket, sorts them, and holds
        out five shillings.*)
ASTON   Here's a few bob.
DAVIES (*taking the coins*) Thank you, thank you, good luck. I just
        happen to find myself a bit short. You see, I got nothing
        for all that week's work I did last week. That's the
        position, that's what it is.
        (*pause*)
ASTON   I went into a pub the other day. Ordered a Guinness. They
        gave it to me in a thick mug. I sat down but I couldn't
        drink it. I can't drink Guinness from a thick mug. I only
        like it out of a thin glass. I had a few sips but I couldn't
        finish it.
        (ASTON *picks up a screwdriver and plug from the bed and begins
        to poke the plug.*)
DAVIES (*with great feeling*) If only the weather would break! Then
        I'd be able to get down to Sidcup!
ASTON   Sidcup?
DAVIES The weather's so blasted bloody awful, how can I get
        down to Sidcup in these shoes?
ASTON   Why do you want to get down to Sidcup?
DAVIES I got my papers there!
        (*pause*)
ASTON   Your what?
DAVIES I got my papers there!
        (*pause*)
ASTON   What are they doing at Sidcup?
DAVIES A man I know has got them. I left them with him. You
        see? They prove who I am! I can't move without them
        papers. They tell you who I am. You see! I'm stuck
        without them.
ASTON   Why's that?
DAVIES You see, what it is, you see, I changed my name! Years
        ago. I been going around under an assumed name! That's
        not my real name.
ASTON   What name you been going under?
DAVIES Jenkins. Bernard Jenkins. That's my name. That's the

name I'm known, anyway. But it's no good me going on
with that name. I got no rights. I got an insurance card
here. (*He takes a card from his pocket.*) Under the name of
Jenkins. See? Bernard Jenkins. Look. It's got four stamps
on it. Four of them. But I can't go along with these. That's
not my real name, they'd find out, they'd have me in the
nick. Four stamps. I haven't paid out pennies. I've paid
out pounds. I've paid out pounds, not pennies. There's
been other stamps, plenty, but they haven't put them on,
the nigs, I never had enough time to go into it.

ASTON They should have stamped your card.

DAVIES It would have done no good! I'd have got nothing
anyway. That's not my real name. If I take that card along
I go in the nick.

ASTON What's your real name, then?

DAVIES Davies. Mac Davies. That was before I changed my name.
(*pause*)

ASTON It looks as though you want to sort all that out.

DAVIES If only I could get down to Sidcup! I've been waiting for
the weather to break. He's got my papers, this man I left
them with, it's got it all down there, I could prove
everything.

Comment and activities

The pacing of the scene and the timing of the actors are crucial to the
effectiveness of this part of the play. Pinter indicates four 'pauses' in
the script; consider what Pinter has to say about silences in the
extract from his speech. Silences say something: they communicate
something about the characters. The air hums with unspoken
communication.

You could see this scene almost as a musical score. Like music it
has its recurring themes and its repetition of phrases. The main
'motif' is the tramp's expression of his need to 'get down to Sidcup'. A
director directing this scene might take that as the main 'statement' of
the scene. Of course, the words suggest more than they actually say.
Davies' desire to get down to Sidcup is an expression of his need to
have some kind of identity, to find some stability in his life, to
establish who he is. His 'papers' will do all those things for him.

Repetition

Davies talks repetitively because he is obsessed by the idea of his papers:

> A man I know has got them. I left them with him. You see? They prove who I am! I can't move without them papers. They tell you who I am. You see! I'm stuck without them.

Round and round Davies' words whirl, always coming back to the same point. One way of playing this would be for the actor to make clear to the audience that Davies is an obsessive, that his papers have a symbolic importance for him. The actor could do this by delivering this speech not to Aston but almost as if he is talking to himself, or some imaginary figure of authority: 'Look here, I am someone, I have an identity, I can't be pushed around, I have my papers. They prove I'm somebody.'

Acting the scene

After talking about the 'few bob' he is to lend Davies, and a pause, Aston talks about what most people would consider to be a very unimportant incident: the mug of Guinness. Dramatically this speech comes from nowhere; nothing in the previous exchanges has led up to it. Notice how precise the words Aston speaks are:

> I went to a pub the other day. Ordered a Guinness. They gave it to me in a thick mug. I sat down but I couldn't drink it. I can't drink Guinness from a thick mug. I only like it out of a thin glass. I had a few sips but I couldn't finish it.

▷   Rehearse the opening section of this scene down to 'I got my papers there.' Decide where the pauses are going to come and which words are going to be stressed, how Davies is going to be played and how Aston's speech about the 'thick mug' is going to be delivered. Then change the parts around and alter the timing and style of delivery in this second version. If Aston's speech was given a restrained, monotonous delivery the first time, for example, try it with a more varied expression this time. Compare the two versions of the scene you have done. Which version did more justice to the language and the sub-text of the scene?

▷   Now that you have tried out a part of the scene, work in groups with one of you acting as the director to perform the whole scene. Take into account the need for silences, the interaction between the two characters, the aim of bringing out the sub-text and the overall timing of the scene. What gestures and expressions would be most appropriate for the two characters in this scene?

Real speech?

▷   In the introduction to 3.6 it was said that Pinter's language echoes real speech, but also goes beyond it to a kind of bleak poetry. Having read and acted this scene, which is typical of Pinter's work, do you agree? Do you think the language is poetic, or is that to elevate it to a level that it does not deserve? Pinter's detractors argue that his plays are pretentious and hollow, pretending to a significance they do not have.

▷   If the language is to be labelled 'poetic', does that effect the way the words are spoken on stage?

▷   Do you think actors need to approach poetry, bleak or otherwise, differently from straight dramatic prose?

3.7   Rhetoric

Rhetoric is the art of using language for persuasion in speaking or writing. John Osborne is a contemporary of Pinter, but he writes about social issues in his plays, or at least, aspects of society that absorb him and which he proceeds to deal with in a public and outward-looking manner. Osborne's leading characters are always in danger of haranguing an audience. As a playwright Osborne does not believe in silences and the sub-text; he unleashes a torrent of words, much of them in a full-blown rhetorical style.

John Osborne, *Look Back in Anger*

Osborne's most famous play is *Look Back in Anger* (1956). When it was first produced, it caused a tremendous amount of controversy and interest. It was hailed as a real breakthrough in British theatre because it was perceived as an antidote to the safe, well-made, basically middle-class play that had dominated British stages for many years.

Osborne's voice, through his anti-hero, Jimmy Porter, was heard as the authentic cry of the disaffected, post-war, grammar-school educated, working-class intellectual railing at the snobberies, complacency and hypocrisy of the out-dated British establishment. The depth of the anger and frustration expressed by Jimmy Porter and the irreverent, almost violent language in which he voiced his attacks,

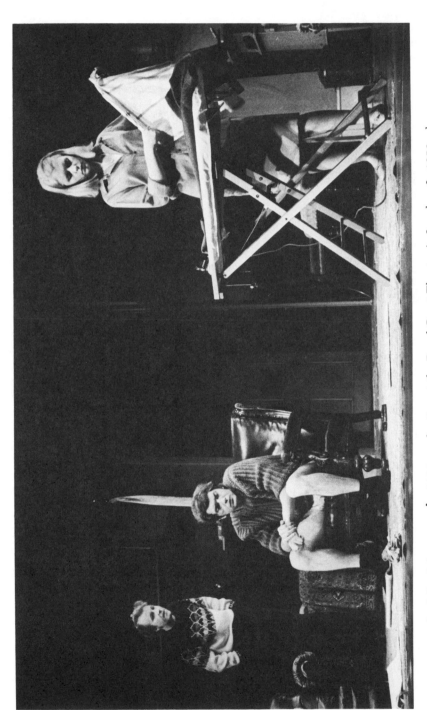

Look Back in anger: the 1968 production at the Royal Court Theatre in London. In 1956 when the play was first produced, it was hailed as the start of a new realism in British theatre.

caused a theatrical sensation. Even the popular press gave the play and its author a lot of attention, dubbing him as the first of the 'angry young men', and his play as the start of a 'kitchen-sink' school of drama.

The success of Osborne's play led to many new dramatists coming to the fore, including Arnold Wesker, John Arden, Harold Pinter, Shelagh Delaney, David Halliwell, Henry Livings, Willis Hall and Ann Jellicoe. These dramatists were very different from one another, but the commercial success of this new type of play encouraged managements to invest in the playwrights. Their success affected other creative arts as well, especially the allied fields of film and television where there was a similar breakthrough in the kind of subjects and characters writers could deal with.

In *Look Back in Anger*, Jimmy Porter, a university graduate from a working-class background, lives with his wife Alison in an attic flat in a Midlands town. They share the flat with Cliff, with whom Jimmy runs a sweet stall in a market. In this extract Helena, an actor friend of Alison's who has been staying with them while she has been appearing in a play in the town, has just persuaded Alison to accompany her to the local church for the Sunday evening service. Jimmy obviously sees this as a betrayal on the part of his wife:

JIMMY   (*to* ALISON) You don't believe in all that stuff. Why you don't believe in anything. You're just doing it to be vindictive, aren't you? Why – why are you letting her influence you like this?

ALISON   (*starting to break*) Why, why, why, why! (*putting her hands over her ears*) That word's pulling my head off!

JIMMY   And as long as you're around, I'll go on using it. (*He crosses down to the armchair, and seats himself on the back of it. He addresses* HELENA'S *back.*)

JIMMY   The last time she was in a church was when she was married to me. I expect that surprises you, doesn't it? It was expediency, pure and simple, We were in a hurry, you see. (*The comedy of this strikes him at once, and he laughs.*) Yes, we were actually in a hurry! Lusting for the slaughter! Well, the local registrar was a particular pal of Daddy's, and we knew he'd spill the beans to the Colonel like a shot. So we had to seek out some local vicar who didn't know him quite so well. But it was no use. When my best man – a chap I'd met in the pub that morning – and I turned up, Mummy and Daddy were in the church already. They'd found out at the last moment, and had come to watch the execution carried out. How I remember looking down at them, full of beer for breakfast, and feeling a bit buzzed. Mummy was slumped over her pew in a heap – the noble, female rhino, pole-axed at last! And Daddy sat beside her, upright and unafraid, dreaming of his days among the Indian Princes, and unable to believe he'd left his horsewhip at home. Just the two of them in that empty church – them and me. (*coming out of his remembrance suddenly*) I'm not sure what happened after that. We must have been married, I suppose. I think I remember being sick in the vestry. (*to* ALISON) Was I?

HELENA   Haven't you finished?
(*He can smell blood again, and he goes on calmly, cheerfully.*)

JIMMY   (*to* ALISON) Are you going to let yourself be taken in by this saint in Dior's clothing? I will tell you the simple truth about her. (*articulating with care*) She is a cow. I wouldn't mind that so much, but she seems to have become a sacred cow as well!

CLIFF   You've gone too far, Jimmy. Now dry up!

HELENA   Oh, let him go on.

JIMMY   (*to* CLIFF) I suppose you're going over to that side as well. Well, why don't you? Helena will help to make it pay off for you. She's an expert in the New Economics – the Economics of the Supernatural. It's all a simple matter of payments and penalties. (*rises*) She's one of those apocalyptic share pushers who are spreading all those rumours about a transfer of power. (*His imagination is racing, and the words pour out.*) Reason and Progress, the old firm, is selling out! Everyone get out while the going's good. Those forgotten shares you had in the old traditions, the old beliefs are going up – up and up and up. (*moves up left*) There's going to be a change over. A new Board of Directors, who are going to see that the dividends are always attractive, and that they go to the right people. (*facing them*) Sell out everything you've got: all those stocks in the old, free inquiry. (*crosses to above table*) The Big Crash is coming, you can't escape it, so get in on the ground floor with Helena and her friends while there's still time. And there isn't much of it left. Tell me, what could be more gilt-edged than the next world! It's a capital gain, and it's all yours.

(*He moves round the table, back to his chair right.*)
You see, I know Helena and her kind so very well. In
fact, her kind are everywhere, you can't move for
them. They're a romantic lot. They spend their time
mostly looking forward to the past. The only place
they can see the light is the Dark Ages. She's moved
long ago into a lovely little cottage of the soul, cut
right off from the ugly problems of the twentieth
century altogether. She prefers to be cut off from all
the conveniences we've fought to get for centuries.
She'd rather go down to the ecstatic little shed at at
the bottom of the garden to relieve her sense of guilt.
Our Helena is full of ecstatic wind – (*he leans across the
table at her*) – aren't you?
(*He waits for her to reply.*)

HELENA   (*quite calmly*) It's a pity you've been so far away all this
time. I would probably have slapped your face.
(*They look into each other's eyes across the table. He moves
slowly up, above* CLIFF, *until he is beside her.*)
You've behaved like this ever since I first came.

JIMMY   Helena, have you ever watched somebody die? (*She
makes a move to rise.*) No, don't move away. (*She
remains seated, and looks up at him.*) It doesn't look
dignified enough for you.

HELENA   (*like ice*) If you come any nearer, I will slap your face.
(*He looks down at her, a grin smouldering round his mouth.*)

Comment and activities

The extract, like most of the play, is dominated by the long speeches
of the main character, Jimmy Porter. The other characters are relegated to the role of responding to his attacks. Dramatically, these
monologues are in danger of creating an inbalance. The subsidiary
roles in this play can be fairly unrewarding for actors.

Reaching out to the audience

The second long speech by Jimmy in this extract is full of rhetorical
flourishes:

> Reason and Progress, the old firm is selling out! Everyone get out
> while the going's good. Those forgotten shares you had in the old
> traditions, the old beliefs are going up – up and up and up.

There is a self-conscious ring to this speech; it is the self-con-

sciousness of the attention-seeking orator. Jimmy might almost be on
a soapbox in the park as in his own living-room. It is rhetoric;
Osborne is using his character to shout his views of society at the
audience. One is left with the impression that the rhetoric is a more
important element than what is happening dramatically among the
characters.

> They're a romantic lot. They spend their time mostly looking
> forward to the past. The only place they can see the light is the
> Dark Ages. She's moved long ago into a lovely little cottage of
> the soul, cut right off from the ugly problems of the twentieth
> century altogether.

Ostensibly the dramatic situation is that Jimmy is attacking Helena as
being representative of a class he hates. But the rhetorical style of the
language inevitably leads to the impression that the dramatist is
haranguing his audience through the mouth of his character. 'Here!'
the author seems to be saying, 'these are my views and you're going to
sit there and listen.'

Acting rhetorical drama

If the whole of *Look Back in Anger* is played at the top of Jimmy
Porter's voice, it becomes tedious. Directors and actors have to find a
way of varying the emotional and vocal pitch. It is, after all, meant to
be a play about the personal and domestic affairs of a small group of
people. Even within this extract there are opportunities for considerable variation. Jimmy's first speech describes his wedding day. He is
performing for everyone's benefit; he is trying to shock. But the
subject of the speech and the description of the day allow the actor to
deliver it in a much less ostentatious and public manner than the
second long speech of the extract.

▷   Work on Jimmy's first long speech in pairs, deciding what is different
     about the language in it as compared to the second long speech. Decide
     what kind of delivery you should use and bear in mind that you want to
     treat this speech in a different way to the second long speech coming up
     shortly in the scene.

▷   The other characters – Alison, Helena and Cliff – play a minor part in the
     scene and yet obviously they are important dramatically if only to throw
     Jimmy into relief by the contrast they provide. Consider the opportunities
     the text provides for the actors playing these parts to underline the

dramatic potential of the scene. Take into account the way they should say their lines, how they should react while Jimmy is launched on his long monologues, and any movements, gestures or expressions that could communicate to the audience how they are feeling.

▷   In rehearsal improvisation can play an important part. Often it is useful to improvise a scene that is described in the play but does not actually take place on stage. The actors are asked to improvise the scene in character and this helps them to understand their characters better. Jimmy Porter gives a very vivid picture of his wedding day in this scene. Choose some details from it and improvise a scene involving Jimmy, Alison and any of the other people mentioned in the account given by Jimmy.

Although Osborne wrote *Look Back in Anger* in a form and style that were seen as different to the 'old-fashioned', well-made play, it actually shares some characteristics with that genre. One of these characteristics is description of action that the audience is not allowed to see and which can only be 'seen' through the eyes of one of the characters (i.e. off-stage action). Jimmy's description of his wedding day is an example of this. Some people consider this to be an undramatic element and a weakness in the play. Why might they think this?

Acting the scene

▷   Act out the whole scene in groups with one person acting as director. Bear in mind the rhetorical style of some of the language and look for ways of varying the vocal pitch used by Jimmy and of involving the 'minor' characters in the scene.

▷   What impression do the speeches of Jimmy Porter make on you? Some people have accused Osborne and his characters of indulging in empty rhetoric. Do you agree or disagree with this view, judging by the extract you have just worked on?

3.8   Checklist and further resources

The following terms and ideas have been used and discussed in this chapter. Check through the list and make sure you know their meaning.

the dramatist's voice   intonation
pure theatre   verse drama

non-verbal theatre   revenge tragedy
naturalism   run-on lines (enjambement)
naturalistic language   end-stop lines
sub-text   rhetoric
high comedy

For modern examples of verse drama see *Ascent of F6* (1936) by W. H. Auden and Christopher Isherwood; *The Dark is Light Enough* (1954) by Christopher Fry.

Short Harold Pinter plays include *The Room* (1957), and *The Dumb Waiter* (1960).

Look Back in Anger (1956) and another play by John Osborne, *Inadmissible Evidence* (1964), have both been filmed, and are frequently screened on television.

For another example of naturalism see *Roots* (1959), by Arnold Wesker.

For another example of Restoration comedy see *Way of the World* (1700) by William Congreve.

4 The audience and the play

A performance of a play requires an audience: indeed, the theatre audience has a great effect on the actual performance. While they are writing plays, dramatists usually have a concept of what kind of audience they hope will eventually see their work. Sometimes they will write plays to set formulas because these have proved successful in the past with certain sections of the theatre-going public.

4.1 Television drama and the audience

The place where most people see plays is their own living room, via the television screen. With one broadcast of a television play, playwrights can reach an audience of millions of people. If the same play were adapted for the stage, it would have to run in a large West End theatre for years to be seen by an equivalent number of people. That measures the drawing-power of television. However, it is generally accepted that television is a more ephemeral medium than the theatre. Only a comparatively few plays written for television survive for long and acquire a lasting reputation.

Writing for television

Writing television drama requires different skills and techniques of the dramatist from writing for the stage. Television is basically a visual medium. It is also a medium that favours realism rather than symbolism or fantasy. Language is perhaps not so important in television drama as it is in stage plays. It could also be claimed that a television audience is open to more manipulation than an audience in a theatre. What is meant by manipulation? Consider this: in a theatre members of an audience can focus their gaze on anything that is happening on stage; they can choose to avert their eyes from the main characters, for example, and watch the actors playing the subsidiary roles. Clearly, those involved in the production will hope to focus the audience's attention where they want it focused, but they cannot control that entirely.

On television, however, the audience has no real choice. The pictures the audience see are chosen for them, shot by shot, cut by cut. The television camera is their third eye, if you like, and this third eye selects, on the instructions of the writer and the director, what the audience is going to see.

Through the use of close-ups the makers of television drama can focus the audience's attention on the slightest of gestures or changes of expression; the camera chooses the details of action and dramatic incident that will register with an audience. Therefore, television dramatists have to write plays with the camera very much in mind. They are not writing for an audience sitting in a theatre. What the audience see on the screen is what is chosen by the writer and the director for the camera to record.

Alan Bleasdale, *Boys from the Blackstuff*

Boys from the Blackstuff (1982) is a quintet of television plays about the lives of a group of unemployed men in Liverpool who, in their desperation to earn a living, moonlight (i.e. take jobs without telling the tax or unemployment authorities, while claiming dole money at the same time).

The extract below is from the first of the plays, *Jobs for the Boys*.

Scene 1   Exterior. Department of Employment Building. Day.
We establish the Department building. A series of shots: two workmen; a girl in white talking to a man; a man with a bucket; the girl in white and the man; a Rastafarian. We see the DOE building. We hear the traffic going past.

Scene 2   Interior. Department of Employment Building. Day.
We see the interior of the DOE. Two general points of view show clerks at work. We see CHRISSIE *and we are aware of the* COUNTER CLERK *who is behind a wire mesh grille. We see* CHRISSIE *and the others in turn through this grille. Like caged animals.*

CLERK	Name.
CHRISSIE	(*misses a beat*) Christopher Todd.
CLERK	Full name. (*takes out a file*)
CHRISSIE	(*quietly*) Christopher Robin Todd. (*shrugs*) It was me Mam. (*turns head*) (*freeze*) (*We see* LOGGO. *He is looking at his gold watch, and is expensively and well dressed.*)
LOGGO	Wha'? Course I want a job. I'm desperate. But look, no offence meant like, but we've been

through all this before an' well, y' have already made
me miss me golf lessons.

CLERK   Look, these matters take time ...

LOGGO   What I'm sayin' is, get a move on, will y', cos I'm
supposed t' be at the Haydock races for half-past two.
There's a good boy.
(*freeze*)
(*We see* YOSSER *with his three children. He is leaning
forward.*)

CLERK   The procedure of a test check is just a formality,
Mr Hughes. However, I'm afraid ...

YOSSER Afraid? Y'll be terrified in a minute. (*leans in*)
Now sort me soddin' Giro check out before I
knock y' into the disability department.
(*freeze*)
(*We see* GEORGE, *who appears to be dressed in working
clothes, but we can only see the top half of him.*)

CLERK   If you could just wait there, Mr Malone ...
(*She goes to a filing cabinet.*)

GEORGE Come on, girl. I should've been on site half an hour
ago.

CLERK   (*hesitant*) Yeah. (*opens filing cabinet*)

GEORGE (*backing away*) I don't like to let the boys down, you
know. I mean, there'll be ten ton of the black stuff on
the deck by now, waitin' for me.
(*We see the* CLERK, *then* GEORGE. *He is wearing pyjama
bottoms and slippers.*)
(*freeze*)
(*A row of men are waiting on a bench. Another row of men
are waiting at the counter. We see* DIXIE.)

CLERK   Dependants, Mr Dean?

DIXIE   Yeah, a wife and four kids. Two at school and two on
the dole.

CLERK   Ah yes, but unfortunately the two on the dole don't
count for ...

DIXIE   No one on the dole counts, friend.
(*freeze*)

Comment and activities

Bleasdale has given clear indications in his script of what he intends
the audience to see on their television screens.

We establish the Department building. A series of shots: two workmen;
a girl in white talking to a man ...

The writer's intention is to give an impression of the DOE building
through a series of shots. Once inside the building, he asks for 'two
general points of view'. The writer wishes to leave the viewers with
the impression of the claimants 'like caged animals'.

Notice how there are no long speeches in the scene: the dialogue is
naturalistic.

Cutting from scene to scene and freezing the picture

The five men – Chrissie, Loggo, Yosser, George and Dixie – are introduced quickly and economically to the viewers by cutting from one
scene to another. This could be done in the theatre as well, but cutting
from scene to scene is much more of a cinematic and television
technique. The freezing of the picture at the end of each short episode
is a way of establishing the identity of the four main characters with
the viewers.

Acting on television

Actors who perform in television drama often bemoan the lack of a
live audience. All television drama is nowadays pre-recorded on
video tape or film. There is no audience for the actors to 'work up
against'.

Another major difference between acting on television and the
stage is the 'size' of the performance required. In the theatre an actor
accommodates his or her gestures and voice projection to the size of
the auditorium. In small theatres where the audience is closer to the
performers, there will not be the same need to project vocally or to
make gestures and expressions much larger than life. Performing in
large theatres, however, is very different; the voice needs to be projected quite a distance and expressions and gestures must be large
enough to be seen by those in the back rows of the upper circle.
Actors in a television studio or on location shooting (when the unit
producing a television drama goes outside the studio to a real
location) have a microphone poised a few inches from them, ready to
take up their merest whisper. A camera can zoom in and record the
slightest facial reaction. Actors can afford to make their performances
'smaller' than in the theatre, and this is why a naturalistic style of
acting often proves best on television.

Acting the scene

▷   It should be an interesting exercise to act two versions of scene 2 from

Jobs for the Boys. One version should be acted as though it is being recorded for showing on television. The second version should be a version for performance in the theatre. What differences in acting techniques will have to be used? How will acting the scene for an imaginary television camera affect the performances of the actors? How will the acting style be different for the stage version? Rehearse the different approaches with a director.

▷   Arrange to watch a television play as a group. Discuss later what specific television techniques were used by the writer, director and actors in the production. What was your own response to the play? Compare the experience of watching a play on television with watching a play on stage.

▷   Write a television version of any of the play extracts you have worked on from this book. Set the script down on paper in the same format as is used for the *Boys from the Blackstuff* extract. You may decide to cut some of the dialogue from the extract you have chosen to adapt and replace it with instructions for the camera. You may want to establish a place or an atmosphere by purely visual means. Think in terms of the television medium when adapting the text.

4.2   The soliloquy and the audience

A soliloquy is a speech which a character in a play makes when he or she is alone on stage. There are two ways of writing and acting soliloquies. The first approach is for the character to speak his or her thoughts aloud, ignoring the presence of the audience. The second approach is for the character to speak directly to the audience, as the Common Man does in the opening section of *A Man for all Seasons* (1.4).

Nikolai Gogol, *The Government Inspector*

Nikolai Gogol brought a kind of comic realism to the Russian theatre of the nineteenth century. Gogol wrote of his play *The Government Inspector* (1836),

> I tried to gather in one heap all that was bad in Russia. I wished to turn it all into ridicule. The real impression produced was that of fear. Through my laughter that I have never laughed more loudly, the spectator feels my bitterness and sorrow.

The Government Inspector: this large-cast comedy lends itself to 'ensemble playing' i.e. each actor playing in the same style as the rest of the cast and avoiding 'star' performances.

The plot of the play depends on the device of mistaken identity, a fairly stock comic situation. A well-dressed nonentity, Hlestakov, arrives in a provincial town with his servant, Yosif, and is mistaken by the town's officials for the Inspector General whom they think has come to investigate official corruption. In this scene from the play, Hlestakov sends Yosif to the landlord of the inn where is he staying, to demand dinner be sent up to him, despite the fact that the landlord has refused to feed him until his bill has been settled. Hlestakov then ponders his situation aloud.

HLESTAKOV   And you enjoy telling me all this, you brute!
YOSIF   He says: 'You people come here, live at ease, run up a bill you can't pay, and then refuse to budge. I'm going straight to the police,' he says, 'with a complaint, and I'm not joking either, and you'll end up in jail.'
HLESTAKOV   That's enough, idiot! Go and tell him, the low animal!

YOSIF   I'd better call him for you to speak to him.
HLESTAKOV   I don't want to see him; go and tell him yourself!
YOSIF   Yes, right, Sir.
HLESTAKOV   Go on, devil take it. Fetch the landlord! (YOSIF
               goes off.) It's awful to be so hungry. I thought I
               could walk it off, but damnation take it, I'm as
               hungry as ever. If only I hadn't had such a spree in
               Penza, there'd have been enough to get home on.
               That infantry captain certainly took me in! The
               way he piled up game after game! The brute! He
               only sat down for a quarter of an hour, but he
               licked me clean. I wish I could have had another go
               at him, but there was no chance. What a dirty little
               hole this town is! These fleabitten shopkeepers
               won't part with anything on tick! A mean lot!
               (*Walks up and down whistling tunes of the day,
               'Roberta,' 'The Marriage of Figaro,' and then anything
               that comes into his head.*)
               (*re-enter* YOSIF *and the* WAITER)
WAITER   The landlord has sent me to ask your pleasure.
HLESTAKOV   Good-day, my friend. How are you?
WAITER   Well, I thank God.
HLESTAKOV   How's the hotel business these days?
WAITER   Very good, God be praised.
HLESTAKOV   Many travellers?
WAITER   Sufficient.
HLESTAKOV   Listen, friend. They've brought me no dinner yet.
               Please hurry up with it, as quickly as possible –
               I've something I must do after dinner.
WAITER   The landlord said he would not serve you anything
               more. He was going to-day to complain to the
               Mayor.
HLESTAKOV   What about? Consider, my dear fellow, I have to
               eat! Or else I should get very thin! I need
               something to eat very badly. I'm not joking!
WAITER   Well, he said: 'I shall serve him no more meals till
               he pays for what he's had'. That was what he said.
HLESTAKOV   You must explain to him, persuade him.
WAITER   But what shall I say?
HLESTAKOV   Well, you must talk to him very seriously, explain
               that I have to eat. The money doesn't matter . . .
               He's a peasant, he thinks it's nothing to go a day
               without eating. A fine idea!

WAITER   All right, I'll tell him. (*exit* WAITER *and* YOSIF)
HLESTAKOV   It'll be frightful, though, if he won't give me
anything to eat! I never knew you could be as
hungry as this before. I might sell some clothes for
ready cash; a few pairs of trousers, say. No! Better
to go hungry than not arrive home in Petersburg
clothes! Pity Joachim wouldn't let me hire that
chaise. It would have been devilish fine to go home
in my own chaise, and go visiting the landowners,
and drive up to the foot of the steps, with the
lanterns burning, and Yosif in livery perched up
behind! I can just imagine everybody getting
excited, and asking, 'Who is it? What is it?' And
the lacquey would go in (*stretching himself and
representing the lacquey*) 'Ivan Alexandrovitch
Hlestakov, from Petersburg; are they at home?'
They're only bumpkins, they wouldn't know what
that meant! If some goose of a landowner went to
see them, he'd charge straight into the drawing-
room like a bear. You make a bee-line for some
pretty daughter. 'Allow me ...' Ugh! It's sickening
to be so hungry!
(*enter* YOSIF, *followed by the* WAITER)
YOSIF   They're bringing some dinner.
HLESTAKOV   (*claps his hands and jumps into a chair*) Dinner!
Dinner! Dinner!

Comment and activities

The actor playing Hlestakov can speak the two soliloquies in this
scene as though he is just thinking aloud (i.e. with no overt acknowl-
edgement that the audience are listening), or he can deliberately take
the audience into his confidence and talk to them directly. The
approach the actor and director take will certainly affect the way in
which the scene is played and the soliloquies are delivered.

The effect of the soliloquy on an audience

If the latter approach is used (i.e. the actor takes the audience into his
or her confidence), then it is likely that the audience will feel closer to
the character than if the character is observed thinking aloud. It
largely depends what effect the director and actor are striving to
achieve – either audience identification with the character, or asking

the audience to distance themselves somewhat from the character, and his or her situation, and judge them both more objectively.

Speaking the soliloquy

The 'thinking aloud' technique will involve the actor in looking as though he or she is verbalising thoughts aloud. The actor should not look directly at the audience or acknowledge their presence. The 'confidential' approach will mean that the actor will look round the audience, perhaps going right down-stage, and will try to include people sitting in all parts of the auditorium in this chat with the audience. The 'confidential' approach will also mean a different vocal delivery from the 'thinking aloud' technique.

▷   Work on both soliloquies in pairs, one person acting as director in turn. Each of you should work on one of the soliloquies, delivering it in the two styles outlined above. As they are longish speeches, you must find ways of varying your delivery in terms of pace, stress, pitch and volume.

Acting the scene

▷   Once you have worked on the soliloquies in pairs, form into larger groups and rehearse the scene as a whole before acting it out.

4.3   The dramatist and the audience

Many people expect the theatre to be purely entertaining rather than disturbing and challenging: any message that a play may have should be secondary to the entertainment value the play provides. Audiences often like to see characters representative of their social class on stage who share their views on society. On the whole, they want to see a flattering portrait of themselves and people like them.

Comedy of manners: Oscar Wilde, *The Importance of Being Earnest*

Oscar Wilde's comedies of manners brought him huge success and fame, before his fall from grace and tragic early death in exile in Paris. Wilde's plays were performed in London to audiences largely composed of upper middle-class people, who recognised, and identified with, the characters and social milieu Wilde portrayed on stage.

His portrait of elegant society is largely flattering. Wilde did poke fun at the mores and social hypocrisies of high society, but the epigrammatic wit and finely-tuned language of his plays helped to create a theatrical image of the class his audiences belonged (or aspired) to, that flattered rather than castigated. Momentarily during the performances of Wilde's plays, audiences of the time might have been disturbed by some social criticism injected by the dramatist, but they could still leave the theatre at the end of the performance with their view of society basically unchanged and their image of themselves reinforced.

The Importance of Being Earnest: this production at the Greenwich Theatre in 1978 emphasises the comedy as taking place against a defined social background.

A century later, with the perspective that social change can give us, and knowing about the inequalities and social injusticies that lay at the heart of Victorian society, we approach Wilde's comedies differently from his contemporary audiences. We can still appreciate the style and the wit, but we can also value the plays as a glimpse into a vanished society. Beneath the surface sophistication, for example, there is an obsession among Wilde's characters with social status, wealth, and what is acceptable behaviour in society.

Below is an extract from the opening scene of *The Importance of Being Earnest* (1895).

> *Morning-room in* ALGERNON'*s flat in Half-Moon Street. The room is luxuriously and artistically furnished. The sound of a piano is heard in the*

adjoining room. LANE *is arranging afternoon tea on the table and, after the music has ceased,* ALGERNON *enters.*

ALGERNON   Did you hear what I was playing, Lane?

LANE   I didn't think it polite to listen, sir.

ALGERNON   I'm sorry for that, for your sake. I don't play accurately – anyone can play accurately – but I play with wonderful expression. As far as the piano is concerned, sentiment is my forte. I keep science for Life.

LANE   Yes, sir.

ALGERNON   And, speaking of the science of Life, have you got the cucumber sandwiches cut for Lady Bracknell?

LANE   Yes, sir. (*hands them on a salver*)

ALGERNON   (*inspects them, takes two, and sits down on the sofa*) Oh! ... by the way, Lane, I see from your book that on Thursday night, when Lord Shoreman and Mr Worthing were dining with me, eight bottles of champagne are entered as having been consumed.

LANE   Yes, sir; eight bottles and a pint.

ALGERNON   Why is it that at a bachelor's establishment the servants invariably drink the champagne? I ask merely for information.

LANE   I attribute it to the superior quality of the wine, sir. I have often observed that in married households the champagne is rarely of a first-rate brand.

ALGERNON   Good heavens! Is marriage so demoralizing as that?

LANE   I believe it *is* a very pleasant state, sir. I have had very little experience of it myself up to the present. I have only been married once. That was in consequence of a misunderstanding between myself and a young person.

ALGERNON   (*languidly*) I don't know that I am much interested in your family life, Lane.

LANE   No, sir; it is not a very interesting subject. I never think of it myself.

ALGERNON   Very natural, I am sure. That will do, Lane, thank you.

LANE   Thank you, sir.
(LANE *goes out.*)

ALGERNON   Lane's views on marriage seem somewhat lax. Really, if the lower orders don't set us a good example, what on earth is the use of them? They seem, as a class, to have absolutely no sense of

moral responsibility.
(*enter* LANE)

LANE Mr Ernest Worthing.
(*enter* JACK, LANE *goes out*)

ALGERNON How are you, my dear Ernest? What brings you up to town?

JACK Oh, pleasure, pleasure! What else should bring one anywhere? Eating as usual, I see Algy!

ALGERNON (*stiffly*) I believe it is customary in good society to take some slight refreshment at five o'clock. Where have you been since last Thursday?

JACK (*sitting down on the sofa*) In the country.

ALGERNON What on earth do you do there?

JACK (*pulling off his gloves*) When one is in town one amuses oneself. When on is in the country one amuses other people. It is excessively boring.

ALGERNON And who are the people you amuse?

JACK (*airily*) Oh, neighbours, neighbours.

ALGERNON Got nice neighbours in your part of Shropshire?

JACK Perfectly horrid! Never speak to one of them.

ALGERNON How immensely you must amuse them!

Comment and activities

Wilde makes his intentions clear right from the start of the play:

ALGERNON Did you hear what I was playing, Lane?

LANE I didn't think it polite to listen, sir.

ALGERNON I'm sorry for that, for your sake. I don't play accurately – anyone can play accurately – but I play with wonderful expression. As far as the piano is concerned, sentiment is my forte. I keep science for Life.

The butler's exaggerated deference in not thinking it polite to listen to his employer's piano-playing makes a gently satirical point about the master–servant relationship and 'polite' society in Wilde's time. Then Algernon, with immense confidence, describes his own talent for piano-playing and throws in an example of epigrammatic wit: 'I keep science for Life'.

Playing comedy of manners

Wilde's plays are usually given stylish productions; that is, a lot of money is spent on costumes and sets. The actors are often encouraged to perform in a rather self-indulgent and 'over the top' manner. Each Wildean epigram is delivered as a separate gem for the audience to delight in, highlighted, rather like a 'hit' number in a musical.

The most interesting recent production of *The Importance of Being Earnest*, Wilde's most famous play, was staged a few years ago at the Greenwich Theatre in London. The production was directed by Jonathan Miller (see 3.1). The actors were encouraged to adopt a more naturalistic style of acting than the usual ostentatious style favoured in most productions of Wilde. The director also tried to place the actors against a defined social context. The play emerged as a strong picture of upper-class London society in a particular period.

Acting the scene

▷   In small groups rehearse two versions of the scene: one version should be acted in a more ostentatious manner while the other version should be more naturalistically played. One member of each group should be the director for both versions. Attention should be paid to the following:

  ○ how the actors interact with one another
  ○ how they deliver the epigrams and comic lines
  ○ how conscious they are of the audience
  ○ how much exaggeration of gesture and manner is used.

▷   When each group has rehearsed both versions, they should present them in front of the group as a whole. Afterwards discuss the differences between the versions of the scene.

4.4   The illusion of reality

Most plays demand of their audiences a suspension of disblief. This involves the audience accepting that what they see on stage for the duration of the play is 'real'. The audience is meant to be so absorbed in the drama that they forget that these are actors on stage, playing parts in a play written by a dramatist.

Catharsis

The audience, it is hoped, will share the emotions of the characters. The ancient Greeks believed that, having experienced the emotions of characters caught up in a tragedy (e.g. the emotions of fear, hatred,

audience would be purged of these emotions
led catharsis. Much British drama demands that
involvement and response.

A photograph from the 1980 National Theatre production of Brecht's historical play, *Galileo*, about the seventeenth-century scientist. Note the sparse sets, characteristic of productions of Brecht's plays. Notice also the projection at the back of the stage which is clearly not the 'real' Padua.

Bertolt Brecht, *St Joan of the Stockyards*

Brecht has already been mentioned in 1.4. His influence on theatrical practice and theory has been very significant. He put forward the theory of the 'alienation effect': the audience should be denied the luxury of wallowing in emotional sympathies for the characters and their situation. They must use their minds to analyse what is being represented on stage. The actors too must have an 'attitude' to the parts they are playing; they must not lose themselves in the parts. Brecht was a political writer; he believed that theatre could help to change people's view of society.

Below is an extract from *St Joan of the Stockyards* (1959). The action is set in the meat-packing plants of Chicago. The workers at the Lennox packing plant revolt against their working conditions and low wages.

In front of the Lennox Plant

THE WORKERS   We are seventy thousand workers in Lennox's
                  packing plant and we
              Cannot live a day longer on such low wages.
              Yesterday our pay was slashed again
              And today the notice is up once more;
              ANYONE NOT SATISFIED
              WITH OUR WAGES CAN GO.
              All right then, let's all go and
              Shit on the wages that get skinnier every day.
              (*a silence*)
              For a long time now this work has made us
                  sick
              The factory our hell and nothing
              But cold Chicago's terrors could
              Keep us here. But now
              By twelve hours' work a man can't even
              Earn a stale loaf and
              The cheapest pair of pants. Now
              A man might just as well go off and
              Die like a beast.
              (*a silence*)
              What do they take us for? Do they think
              We are going to stand here like steers, ready
              For anything? Are we
              Their chumps? Better lie and rot!
              Let's go right now.
              (*a silence*)
              It must be six o'clock by now!
              Why don't you open up, you sweatshop
                  bosses? Here
              Are your steers, you butchers, open up!
              (*They knock.*)
              Maybe they've forgotten us?
              (*laughter*)
              Open the gates! We
              Want to get into your
              Dirt-holes and lousy kitchens
              To cook stuffed meat
              For the eaters who possess.
              (*a silence*)
              We demand at least

	Our former wages, even though they were too low, at least
	A ten–hour day and at least –
A MAN	*(crossing the stage)*
	What are you waiting for? Don't you know
	That Lennox has shut down?
	(NEWSBOYS *run across the stage.*)
THE NEWSBOYS	Meat king Lennox forced to shut down his plants! Seventy thousand workers without food or shelter! M. L. Lennox a victim of bitter competitive struggle with Pierpont Mauler, well-known meat baron and philanthropist.
THE WORKERS	Alas!
	Hell itself
	Shuts its gate in our faces!
	We are doomed. Bloody Mauler grips
	Our exploiter by the throat and
	We are the ones who choke!

A Street

THE NEWSBOYS	Chicago Tribune, noon edition! P. Mauler, meat baron and philanthropist, to attend opening of the P. Mauler Hospitals, largest and most expensive in the world!
	(P. MAULER *passes, with two men.*)
A PASSER-BY	*(to another)* That's P. Mauler. Who are the men walking with him?
THE OTHER	Detectives. They guard him so that he won't be knocked down.

Comment and activities

Brecht makes the workers speak in unison as a 'chorus' to the audience. There is nothing new about having a chorus – classical Greek drama used one very often. The chorus probably appealed to Brecht because it enables groups of actors to address the audience directly. Choral speaking is not a naturalistic device; Brecht reacted against naturalism. He believed in using theatrical devices and language, but not in the service of lulling an audience into believing in the reality of what was taking place on stage.

Choral speaking

The chorus speaks in verse: the rhythm of the language is clearly very important. First, however, the meaning and emotional content of the text need to be analysed. Strong emotions are expressed in the lines below:

> THE WORKERS   For a long time now this work has made us
> sick
> The factory our hell and nothing
> But cold Chicago's terrors could
> Keep us here.

Words like 'made us sick', 'our hell' and 'cold Chicago's terrors' cannot be spoken neutrally or without emotional conviction by the chorus. The choral speaking must reflect the dramatic situation and the emotions of the workers. This has to be stressed because some choral speaking emphasises clear diction and a 'sing-song' effect at the expense of the meaning of the words. Clear diction is, nevertheless, a very important part of choral speaking on stage.

In addition to emotional conviction, clarity, and speaking in unison, good choral speaking requires variation in pitch, tone, volume and stress. Not all the choruses need be spoken by the entire group – some short sections can be spoken by a group within the chorus, or by individual members.

▷   In groups of four or five, discuss how each of the choruses could be delivered. Mark the points in the text where individual words or phrases have to be stressed, the pace of the delivery quickened or slowed, the volume raised or lowered and where a variation of tone could be employed. If one or two voices can deliver a short section rather than the whole chorus, mark those points as well.

▷   Having discussed them, rehearse each of the choruses until each group has achieved a satisfactory level of performance.

Acting the scene

▷   Now add the other elements of the scene: the knocking at the factory door and the laughter, the passer-by and the newsboys. Act the whole scene.

4.5   Theatre Workshop

Brecht has had an undoubted influence on theatre in many countries. A similar style was developing in parts of Britain, the most significant of which was the Theatre Workshop, which grew up in Lancashire in the early thirties. It called upon popular traditions and was regarded at the time as subversive. It led to the work of Joan Littlewood and her Theatre Workshop which eventually settled in the East End of London. The peak of the Theatre Workshop's artistic achievement and fame was reached in the 1950s and early 1960s. One of Littlewood's prime aims was to bring working-class audiences back to the theatre. The Theatre Royal in Stratford in East London was her base; she rejected the glamour of London's West End theatres to concentrate on her work with her various companies of actors in a small theatre in an unfashionable area of the capital. Several of the shows she produced in the Theatre Royal were transferred to West End theatres where they had successful runs and won critical acclaim.

The style of Littlewood's productions was rumbustious, irreverent and free-wheeling. She wanted to entertain audiences as well as enlighten them politically. She and her actors employed techniques and skills arising out of the old music-hall tradition, musical comedy and the circus. Actors were encouraged to use any skill they had: song-and-dance, juggling, stand-up comic patter, mime and improvisation. Total theatre was one of the concepts that lay behind much of their work. Theatre had to harness aspects of all the performing arts to entertain, and communicate with, an audience.

Audiences in the music halls were frequently encouraged to sing along and to join in comic banter with the performers. Similarly, Theatre Workshop's audiences were meant to be an integral part of the performance. Going to the theatre was meant to be fun and not a solemn ritual.

Oh What a Lovely War

One of the most famous productions of the Theatre Workshop was *Oh What a Lovely War* (1963). This was a kind of chronicle of the First World War, viewed from the perspective of ordinary soldiers and their families. The show uses songs and official documents of the period. Littlewood and her company set themselves the task of translating this material into theatrical terms i.e. using any theatrical means available to bring the material to life.

Below is an extract from *Oh What a Lovely War*. The stage

is set as for a pierrot seaside show of fifty years ago, with red, white and blue fairy lights, and coloured circus tubs which are used as seats throughout the play. Above the stage there is a newspanel across which messages are flashed during the action. There is also a screen behind the acting area, onto which slides are projected. In the extract, the pierrot group are about to present their show. The Master of Ceremonies (M.C.) introduces it ...

BAND	*March of the Gladiators*
	(Circus Parade: two pierrot-acrobats lead on the company dressed in national costumes. A French group of three pierrots – one man (a French army officer), two women; a German group – the Kaiser and a woman, Austria; a British group of five – a woman, Ireland, leading, a British colonial on the shoulders of another, followed by a fan-holder, and a coloured servant; Russian group of two men. The company move round the stage in a circle as in a circus parade, finally stopping, keeping the circular shape, when the German group is downstage centre on the second time round.
NEWSPANEL	Troops fire on Dublin crowd – Aug 1 British cabinet vote against helping France if war comes – Liberals vote for neutrality under any circumstances – Germany sends 40,000 rifles to Ulster.
M.C.	*(as the nations pass)* La Belle France – Upright, steadfast Germany – Good morning, sir – The first part of the game is called 'Find the Thief'.
BAND	*Sons of the Sea*
BRITAIN	Look here, we own 30 million square miles of colonies. The British Empire is the most magnificent example of working democracy the world has ever seen.
VOICE	Hear absolutely hear.
M.C.	And the lady on my right.
BAND	*Si le Vin est Bon*
FRENCHWOMAN	La République
FRENCHMAN	The seat of reason, the centre of world civilisation – culture, and l'amour.
M.C.	They're at it again. Stop it. If they're not doing that, they're eating. How big's your acreage?

FRENCHWOMAN	Six million square kilometres.
M.C.	And you?
BAND	*German music*
KAISER	Germany – a mere three million square kilometres. But we are a new nation united only since 1871.
FRENCHWOMAN	When you stole Alsace-Lorraine.
KAISER	Ours, German.
M.C.	Hey, we haven't started to play the game yet.
KAISER	We are a disciplined, moral, industrious people. We want more say in the world's affairs.
M.C.	Have to keep an eye on you ... (*to the band*) Let's have the Russian anthem. You're in the three-mile limit. You're all right.
BAND	*Russian anthem*
RUSSIAN	They're all yids.
NEWSPANEL	Churchill orders fleet to Scapa Flow.
M.C.	(*to audience*) The second part of the War Game. The Plans.
BAND	*German music*
KAISER	War is unthinkable. It is out of the question.
FRENCHMAN	It would upset the balance of power.
BRITAIN	It would mean the ruin of the world, undoubtedly.
FRENCHMAN	Besides, our alliances make us secure.
KIASER	But if you threaten us, then we have the supreme deterrent, which we will not hesitate to use ...
M.C.	Ssh ... secret
	(*The* M.C. *whistles. The stage darkens and the screen comes down. Everyone leaves but the* KAISER *and* AUSTRIA. GENERAL MOLTKE *enters.* RUSSIA, FRANCE, *and* BRITAIN *listen at the doors.*)
SLIDE 1	*Map showing the Schlieffen plan of 1914 for an attack on Paris.*
MOLTKE	The German Army will win this battle by an envelopment with the right wing, and let the last man brush the Channel with his sleeve.
KAISER	Violate the neutrality of Belgium and the Netherlands?
MOLTKE	World power or downfall. Liège twelve days

after mobilization M. Day, Brussels M.19,
French frontier M.22, and we will enter Paris
at 11.30 on the morning of M.39. I send all the
best brains in the War College into the
Railway Section.

KAISER   And the Russians?

MOLTKE   They won't be ready till 1916.

Oh What a Lovely War: total theatre in the style of Joan littlewood's Theatre
Workshop. Their aim was to entertain audiences *and* make people think.

Comment and activities

Theatrical means

The term 'total theatre' can be used to describe *Oh What a Lovely War*
(see 1.4). The production calls for movement, acrobatics, costume,
music, pageantry, newspanels, screens and slide projection, as well
as tremendous versatility from the actors. The technology –

e.g. the newspanel – is not absolutely vital to a production of the play; the most essential tools directors and actors need are imagination and resourcefulness.

For example, the newspanel can be replaced by two news-vendors on opposite sides of the stage, shouting the latest news, 'Troops fire on Dublin crowd.' The music for the show can be recorded. The screen and slides could be replaced by ready-made diagrams that could be whisked on and off stage.

The essence of Theatre Workshop's kind of theatre is improvisation – many of the words actors speak are improvised in rehearsal. Everything in a Theatre Workshop production has to be conceived in theatrical terms.

Directing 'total theatre'

The director's role in a total theatre production is to integrate the different strands into a coherent theatrical entertainment. However, the theatricality of the show must not swamp the drama as such. *Oh What a Lovely War* is making a serious point about the exploitation of ordinary people. If all the acting versatility, the songs and dances, the razzmatazz, the spectacle and the excitement of the production somehow blot out the dramatic qualities of the piece, then all those theatrical means have been used largely in vain. A director has to keep a tight rein on the proceedings and allow the drama to make its point to an audience.

Acting the scene

▷   To act this scene, you will need some simple props to symbolise, for example, pierrots and national identities. As a group decide how you are going to replace the Newspanel. Choose some suitable music (it need not be the music mentioned in the text).

▷   What kind of acting style are you going to use? These characters are representative figures – you can afford to make them quite 'large'. This show depends on making a direct appeal to an audience. Add ideas of your own about how to communicate the point of the text to an audience.

4.6   Political theatre

The theatre has always had the capacity to deal with contemporary social and political issues. After all, it is a live medium: what happens in social and political life during the day can be turned into drama on stage in the evening. The fringe or alternative theatre often incorporates into shows and plays references to immediate political topics. Some dramatists are committed to particular political or social beliefs in their plays. These committed dramatists run the danger of writing heavy-handed, polemical plays which leave audiences feeling they have been lectured by the playwright and that he or she has used the stage as a soapbox. On the other hand, however, some audiences seem to like their beliefs and prejudices confirmed for them in the theatre.

This theatrical affirmation of what an audience are already convinced about, occurs in plays of various political hues. Left-wing and right-wing audiences are both equally likely to have their opinions massaged in the theatre.

Dramatists can be politically-committed writers without preaching or being overtly one-sided. For example, they can avoid creating dramatic ciphers either for the characters who represent the views they approve of, or the characters who are the enemies of those ideas. The conflicting protagonists can be equally matched so that the 'good guys' (from the playwright's point of view) do not outdraw the 'bad guys' with such consummate ease that the victory of the 'right' side is perceived as dramatically empty.

Trevor Griffiths, *The Party*

Trevor Griffiths is generally seen as a playwright committed to socialist ideals. His plays, however, are not overtly preaching. His left-wing characters are frequently flawed human beings and their opponents are not portrayed as devils incarnate or stage villains.

Below is an extract from Griffiths' play *The Party* (1973). It consists of part of a dialogue between Tagg, a long-time left-wing activist and a full-time organiser for the Revolutionary Socialist Party, and Joe, a television producer who is a disenchanted socialist. The play is set in 1968, when there was social and political great turmoil in many European countries, particularly in France. A meeting has just ended which has been attended by representatives of various left-wing factions; the meeting has been about the strategy which the revolutionary Left in Britain should take in relation to the current upheavals.

>   JOE   I'm sorry the meeting ... wasn't better.
> TAGG   It's a start (*Pause.* TAGG *sinks into himself.*)
>   JOE   Don't you have ... doubts?
> TAGG   Doubts?
>   JOE   I've been trying to figure out what makes you different.

It's not your analysis. It's not your style either. I think it's
... there's no ... scepticism in you. I can find no trace of
what my psychology tutor used to call 'the civilised
worm' in you, gently insisting on the possibility of error.
(*pause*) Perhaps it's just that you have no way of being
wrong.

TAGG   (*softly*) Do *you* have a way of being right?

JOE   No. I don't.

TAGG   I'm not afraid of being wrong. As long as I'm right just
once. That's all it'll take.
(*silence*)
(*smiling briefly*) I'm proletarian. I killed the worm before it
turned. (*he takes in the room, piece by piece, then back to* JOE)
Mebbe you should've done the same.

JOE   Me? I'm just a .. producer. I don't actually *do* anything.
I just ... set up the shows.
(*silence again*)

TAGG   I met Trotsky, you know. Just the once. In a pension in
southern France. '36. '36 I think it was. He was trying to
set up the Fourth International to counter the obscenities
of Stalin's Third. There were about fifty of us, from all
over: France, Italy, Switzerland, Belgium, Holland,
Germany, Sweden, Denmark ... Poland ... Australia ...
America. And me, from Glasgow. Just thirty. (*pause*) He
spoke mainly in French. I barely understood a word. But
I watched him. Watched him. His big head. His eyes
behind the spectacles. (*pause*) Authentic. This voice,
speaking a language I didna comprehend, was the sole
remaining authentic voice of the Russian revolution.
While just about everything else was being expunged by
Stalin or just ... papered over by the Wilsons of their day
... this one burning intelligence sat there refusing to be
quenched, to be put out. (*long pause*) It's helped, that. Of
course, it's no substitute for analysis and argument, for
theory. But it helps a wee bit when the nights start getting
longer. (*pause*) He said one thing I did understand. He
said: 'We only die when we fail to take root in others.'
(*silence for a long time*)
I'm trying to take root, Joe. (*pause*) I'll be dead by the end
of the year. (*pause*) I have this tumour. (*He holds his
stomach.*) They've been trying to treat it for a while now,
you know. But it's ... spread just the same. I was there
tonight. That's why I was late.

JOE   I'm sorry ...
TAGG (*completely naturally*) Ach, it's nothing. It's just such a
      bloody waste. I was banking on ten more good years to
      build the party.
JOE   Are there ... dependents?
TAGG No. (*He stands up suddenly, a hard, stern lump.*) We'll meet
      again, eh?
JOE   (*standing too*) Yes.
      (TAGG *holds his hand out.* JOE *takes it.*)
      Let me call a cab.

Comment and activities

Contrasting characters

Actors performing a scene together on stage can help each other
establish the character each is playing by taking the opportunites
presented by the playwright for contrasting characterisation. In the
scene above there is an obvious contrast between the characters.

Tagg is clear and definite in his views. He is unswerving in his
devotion to the cause. He also speaks with a Glaswegian accent. An
actor preparing to play this role does not only have to study the words
he will speak as the character but also what *is said* by other characters
about him.
Thus, what Joe says about Tagg:

> There's no ... scepticism in you. I can find no trace of what my
> psychology tutor used to call 'the civilised worm' in you, gently
> insisting on the possibility of error.

is important evidence about the impression Tagg makes on people,
and should help the actor in his preparation for playing the character.
Joe is a contrast to Tagg. There are clues in his words to Tagg:

> Don't you have ... doubts?

> Me? I'm just a ... producer. I don't actually *do* anything. I just ...
> set up the shows.

He is unsure of himself. He feels impotent.
A director and the actors should discuss the possiblities for contrast
in the playing of the two characters.

Varying the tone

Tagg has one long speech in the scene. The actor has to find a variation in pace, tone, stress and pitch within the speech, otherwise it could become monotonous in delivery. The dramatist has indicated numerous pauses, one long pause and 'silence for a long time'. The timing of these pauses and the dramatic effect they are meant to achieve are crucial to the delivery of the speech. The speech leads to a kind of climax when Tagg admits to a human weakness – he has cancer and is dying. The implacable revolutionary shows a human face. The dramatist has presented the actor playing Tagg with the chance to uncover another layer of this man's character.

Acting the scene

▷   Work in pairs on Tagg's long speech. Look for ways of varying the delivery. Consider how Tagg would announce the news that he is dying. Take it in turns to direct one another in preparing this speech for performance. (Do not worry about Tagg's Glaswegian accent, if this proves any difficulty.)

Having worked on the long speech and discussed how to convey the contrast between the two characters, divide into groups of three to act out the scene, with one person taking on the director's role.

Further discussion

▷   Have you ever seen any political theatre where the performance seems to be committed to, or arguing for, a particular political point of view? What was your reaction to it? Should dramatists take a 'balanced' view of political issues in their plays? Does political theatre necessarily mean off-putting and preaching plays?

4.7   Checklist and further resources

The following terms and ideas have been used and discussed in this chapter. Check through the list and make sure you know their meaning.

manipulation	suspension of disbelief
cutting	catharsis
voice projection	chorus
soliloquy	total theatre
comedy of manners	political theatre
epigram	

For a modern comedy which deals with social and political issues see *The Ruling Class* (1968) by Peter Barnes.

A film version of *The Importance of Being Earnest* by Oscar Wilde is available. See also the plays/films of Noel Coward (1899-1973).

Other relevant plays by Bertolt Brecht include *Mother Courage and her Children* (1941); and *The Caucasian Chalk Circle* (1954).

A film version of *Oh What a Lovely War*, directed by Richard Attenborough, is available.

For a further example of Trevor Griffiths' work, see *The Comedians* (1975).

5   Genres

The theatre has established 'genres' or types of plays, each of which has its own stock elements and characters, situations and stage conventions. London's West End theatres, for example, rely on a continuous diet of musicals, whodunnits, farces and comedies. Occasionally a historical drama or play dealing with a social issue are produced, and these too fit into well-tried categories of genre productions.

The criticism of the commercial theatre's dependence on such genres is that it leads to very unadventurous productions. On the other hand, audiences paying for expensive seats want to ensure they are going to enjoy themselves on their night out at the theatre and so tend to book for the types of productions that have entertained them in the past.

5.1   Working creatively within genres

The conventions of theatrical genres need not necessarily be a strait-jacket on the talents of writers, actors and directors. These conventional elements can be used imaginatively. Musicals such as *West Side Story* and *Cabaret* prove that the conventions of the American musical, for example, can be employed to create very worth-while entertainment. Anthony Shaffer's *Sleuth* may have sent up the conventions of the British country-house thriller, but it manages to provide an intelligent evening at the theatre in doing so. Robert Bolt's *A Man for all Seasons* (1.4) uses many of the elements of the conventional historical drama, but they are used imaginatively to produce an admirable play.

Thus, working within the various theatrical genres need not spell death to genuine creativity. In this chapter extracts from five plays which have conventional genre elements will be looked at.

5.2   Shakespearian revenge tragedy

In the late sixteenth and early seventeenth centuries, Shakespeare wrote plays that belonged to established genres of the period. Elizabethan and Jacobean audiences were accustomed to certain conven-

tional theatrical forms and had definite expectations of certain types
of plays. In his tragedy *Hamlet*, Shakespeare has one of his characters, Polonius, mention all the various genres familiar to the theatre-
going public of the time:

> The best actors in the world, either for tragedy, comedy, history,
> pastoral, pastoral–comical, historical–comical, tragical–comical–
> historical–pastoral . . .

Of course, Shakespeare here is making fun of the many mixed genres
of his time, but he often worked within accepted genres, accepting
conventional elements and types of characters, but attempting, and
succeeding in, breathing new life into them.

In Shakespeare's time, a tragedy dealt with the destruction of a
great figure through a combination of fate and the flaws in his own
character. (Virtually all the main protagonists at this time were male.)
'Revenge tragedy' was a sub-genre within the wider genre of tragedy.
In a revenge tragedy, the hero was given a task of revenge which he
was compelled by honour and tradition to carry out. The revenge
tragedy follows the hero's progress in carrying out this revenge which
invariably costs him his life. Conventional elements included ghosts
and the supernatural, thwarted love, disguise and mistaken identity,
madness, multiple deaths, duels, gore, torture, a play-within-a-play,
scenes of comic relief and the ultimate destruction of the avenging
hero.

William Shakespeare, *Hamlet*

Shakespeare used most of the elements of the revenge tragedy in
Hamlet (c. 1602). Working within a conventional genre, he managed
to produce one of his greatest plays.

In the extract below, Hamlet, the Prince of Denmark, has come to
meet Horatio and Marcellus on the ramparts of Elsinore Castle. His
friends have reported to Hamlet that they have seen the ghost of
Hamlet's father, the previous king, walking the ramparts after midnight. Hamlet is in a melancholy state after the death of his father and
due to the fact that his uncle rather than himself has been chosen to
succeed to the throne; he is also upset by the hasty marriage of his
mother, the widowed queen, to his uncle.

A flourish of trumpets, and two pieces go off.

HORATIO   What does this mean, my lord?
HAMLET   The King doth wake tonight and takes his rouse,

Keeps wassail, and the swagg'ring upspring reels,
And as he drains his draughts of Rhenish down
The kettledrum and trumpet thus bray out
The triumph of his pledge.

HORATIO   Is it a custom?

HAMLET   Ay, marry, is't,
But to my mind, though I am native here
And to the manner born, it is a custom
More honored in the breach than the observance.
This heavy-headed revel east and west
Makes us traduced and taxed of other nations.
They clepe us drunkards and with swinish phrase
Soil our addition, and indeed it takes
From our achievements, though performed at
    height,
The pith and marrow of our attribute.
So oft it chances in particular men
That for some vicious mole of nature in them,
As in their birth, wherein they are not guilty,
(Since nature cannot choose his origin)
By the o'ergrowth of some complexion,
Oft breaking down the pales and forts of reason,
Or by some habit that too much o'erleavens
The form of plausive manners, that (these men,
Carrying, I say, the stamp of one defect.
Being nature's livery, or fortune's star)
Their virtues else, be they as pure as grace,
As infinite as man may undergo,
Shall in the general censure take corruption
From that particular fault. The dram of evil
Doth all the noble substance of a doubt,
To his own scandal.
(enter GHOST)

HORATIO   Look, my lord, it comes.

HAMLET   Angels and ministers of grace defend us!
Be thou a spirit of health or goblin damned,
Bring with thee airs from heaven or blasts from
    hell,
Be thy intents wicked or charitable,
Thou com'st in such a questionable shape
That I will speak to thee. I'll call thee Hamlet,
King, father, royal Dane. O, answer me!
Let me not burst in ignorance, but tell

Why thy canonisèd bones, hearsèd in death,
Have burst their cerements, why the sepulcher
Wherein we saw thee quietly interred
Hath oped his ponderous and marble jaws
To cast thee up again. What may this mean
That thou, dead corse, again in complete steel,
Revisits thus the glimpses of the moon,
Making night hideous, and we fools of nature
So horridly to shake our disposition
With thoughts beyond the reaches of our souls?
Say, why is this? Wherefore? What should we do?
(GHOST *beckons* HAMLET)

HORATIO   It beckons you to go away with it,
As if it some impartment did desire
To you alone.

MARCELLUS   Look with what courteous action
It waves you to a more removèd ground.
But do not go with it.

HORATIO   No, by no means.

HAMLET   It will not speak. Then I will follow it.

HORATIO   Do not, my lord.

HAMLET   Why, what should be the fear?
I do not set my life at a pin's fee,
And for my soul, what can it do to that,
Being a thing immortal as itself?
It waves me forth again. I'll follow it.

HORATIO   What if it tempt you toward the flood, my lord,
Or to the dreadful summit of the cliff
That beetles o'er his base into the sea,
And there assume some other horrible form,
Which might deprive your sovereignty of reason
And draw you into madness? Think of it.
The very place puts toys of desperation,
Without more motive, into every brain
That looks so many fathoms to the sea
And hears it roar beneath.

HAMLET   It waves me still.
Go on; I'll follow thee.

MARCELLUS   You shall not go, my lord.

HAMLET   Hold off your hands.

HORATIO   Be ruled. You shall not go.

HAMLET   My fate cries out
And makes each petty artere in this body

As hardy as the Nemean lion's nerve.
Still am I called! Unhand me, gentlemen.
By heaven, I'll make a ghost of him that lets me!
I say, away! Go on. I'll follow thee.
(*exit* GHOST, *and* HAMLET)

Comment and activities

A director often has an overall concept of a play, an interpretation of
the play's themes that he or she wishes to stress in the playing of it.
Hamlet has always been the target for such directorial interpretation
because of its complexity and ambiguities.

The hero, Hamlet, has been played in many different ways by a
legion of actors. He can be played as the dithering intellectual, the
neurotic adolescent in love with his own mother, the thwarted and
melancholic lover, the Renaissance prince brought low by his own
indecision, the weakling, or the philosopher man-of-action.

Hamlet: The production of the Citizens' Company, Glasgow in 1981. Of all
Shakespeare's plays, *Hamlet* is the target for unconventional interpretations in
the search to shed new light on the text.

'Pointing' a speech or a scene

If a director has a particular interpretation he or she wants to convey,
then it is quite usual for a particular scene or speech to receive special

'pointing', or stress. In the extract above there is a speech by Hamlet in which the character, without realising it, analyses his own failings — the fatal flaw in his character:

> So oft it chances in particular men
> That for some vicious mole of nature in them ...
>
> Carrying, I say, the stamp of one defect;
>
> Shall in the general censure take corruption
> From that particular fault.

If a director decides on the 'fatal flaw' interpretation of Hamlet, then obviously this speech is very important to that interpretation. The director and actor are going to work out a method of pointing this speech so that its importance to the understanding of the character and the themes of the play is communicated to the audience.

Moves on stage

Sometimes a speech can be given an emphasis by the simple devices of a pause and a move on stage. For example, before Hamlet starts on the 'vicious mole of nature' train of thought, he has been talking about the drunken reputation Danes are acquiring among other nations. If a director wishes to give extra emphasis to the rest of this speech, he or she could make the actor pause and move down stage. This would isolate the 'fatal flaw' section from the rest and give it emphasis from an audience's point of view.

In addition, this section of the long speech could be delivered in a more pensive and inward-looking manner by the actor playing Hamlet, as though he were half-conscious that he himself suffered from 'the stamp of one defect'.

▷   In pairs work on the speech 'Ay, marry, is't ...' Decide how you are going to underline the importance of the 'vicious mole of nature' theme by the use of pauses, moves and variation of delivery. Rehearse the speech, then act it out.

The ghost

Shakespeare's audiences would have expected a fully-fledged ghost with all the supernatural trimmings to appear on stage in the scene above. People of the time believed in spirits and the supernatural more readily than most people today. For modern audiences, the appearance of ghosts on stage is more problematical. Not many productions of *Hamlet* nowadays accompany the ghost's appearance with eerie music, creeping fog from dry ice, screeching owls and other clichés of theatrical supernatural effects.

▷   But it is a problem for directors and actors how best to present the ghost of Hamlet's father on stage. Should the ghost be played naturalistically? Or should the director emphasise the ghostly effects and attempt to create a supernatural atmosphere?
Discuss these alternative approaches in groups, then work on the scene in which the ghost appears, having made up your mind how it should be presented.

Variation of tone and delivery

Within this scene, Hamlet is seen to be caustic, philosphical, horror-struck, fearless and determined. The scene demands a lot from the actor in terms of variation of tone and delivery. An actor preparing for this scene might well mark the text in this way:

The King doth wake tonight
      (bitter tone)

And to my mind, though I am native here
      (saddened, ashamed)

So oft it chances ...
*(pensive, almost as if speaking
                    to himself)*
Angels and minsters of grace defend us!
      (horror-struck)

I do not set my life at a pin's fee
      (wild, crazy)

▷   There are other points in the scenes where tone and delivery could be varied apart from these. In groups, analyse Hamlet's speeches and decide where an actor needs to alter tone, pace and delivery.

Acting the scene

▷   Once you have worked on these different aspects of the scene, divide into groups and act the scene. One of the group should take the role of director.

5.3 Modern tragedy

The tragic heroes of Shakespeare's plays, and those of his contemporary dramatists, were almost without exception figures of importance and status in the world: kings, princes, generals, members of the aristocracy.

The subjects of modern tragedy are usually much more ordinary people. The heroes of modern tragedy most often belong to the middle-class. Fate plays a lesser role in modern tragedy; usually modern tragic heroes are destroyed by their own drives towards impossible dreams of success and material wealth.

Anti-heroes

It is perhaps a mistake to refer to the 'heroes' of modern tragedy, because the hero has been replaced largely by the anti-hero in twentieth-century drama. We are less prone to believe in individuals of outstanding merit and virtues, in an age when we pride ourselves on understanding human motivation and capacity for destruction and evil.

Arthur Miller, *Death of a Salesman*

Arthur Miller is a contemporary American playwright who has written several plays which can be classed as modern tragedies. His 'heroes' are very ordinary men, usually middle-class, who are brought low by their pursuit of the prizes offered through the 'American Dream' – status, success and wealth, and power. In his most famous play, *Death of a Salesman* (1949), Miller chooses Willy Loman, a salesman, as his main protagonist. He is a man who has lived his life in the fruitless quest for the riches and status he thinks are there for the picking by the person who applies himself to achieving success and making the right friends.

In this extract from the play, Willy is pleading with Howard, the young boss of the firm by which Willy is employed, for a job in the office. Willy is a burnt-out, exhausted salesman who can no longer sell anything.

> WILLY   I tell ya why, Howard. Speaking frankly and between the two of us, y'know – I'm just a little tired.
>
> HOWARD   Oh, I could understand that, Willy. But you're a road man, Willy, and we do a road business. We've only got a half-dozen salesmen on the floor here.

WILLY   God knows, Howard, I never asked a favour of any
           man. But I was with the firm when your father used
           to carry you in here in his arms.
HOWARD   I know that, Willy, but . . .
WILLY   Your father came to me the day you were born and
           asked me what I thought of the name of Howard,
           may he rest in peace.
HOWARD   I appreciate that, Willy, but there just is no spot here
           for you. If I had a spot I'd slam you right in, but I just
           don't have a single solitary spot.
           (*He looks for his lighter;* WILLY *has picked it up and gives
           it to him. Pause.*)
WILLY   (*with increasing anger*) Howard, all I need to set my
           table is fifty dollars a week.
HOWARD   But where am I going to put you, kid?
WILLY   Look, it isn't a question of whether I can sell
           merchandise, is it?
HOWARD   No, but it's a business, kid, and everybody's gotta
           pull his own weight.
WILLY   (*desperately*) Just let me tell you a story, Howard . . .
HOWARD   'Cause you gotta admit, business is business.
WILLY   (*angrily*) Business is definitely business, but just listen
           for a minute. You don't understand this.. When I was
           a boy – eighteen, nineteen – I was already on the
           road. And there was a question in my mind as to
           whether selling had a future for me. Because in those
           days I had a yearning to go to Alaska. See, there were
           three gold strikes in one month in Alaska, and I felt
           like going out. Just for the ride, you might say.
HOWARD   (*barely interested*) Don't say.
WILLY   Oh, yeah, my father lived many years in Alaska. He
           was an adventurous man. We've got quite a little
           streak of self-reliance in our family. I thought I'd go
           out with my older brother and try to locate him, and
           maybe settle in the North with the old man. And I
           was almost decided to go, when I met a salesman in
           the Parker House. His name was Dave Singleman.
           And he was eighty-four years old, and he'd drummed
           merchandise in thirty-one states. And old Dave, he'd
           go up to his room, y'understand, put on his green
           velvet slippers – I'll never forget – and pick up his
           phone and call the buyers, and without ever leaving
           his room, at the age of eighty-four, he made his
           living. And when I saw that, I realized that selling

was the greatest career a man could want. 'Cause
what could be more satisfying than to be able to go,
at the age of eighty-four, into twenty or thirty
different cities, and pick up a phone, and be
remembered and loved and helped by so many
different people? Do you know? when he died – and
by the way he died the death of a salesman, in his
green velvet slippers in the smoker of the New York,
New Haven, and Hartford, going into Boston –
when he died, hundreds of salesmen and buyers were
at his funeral. Things were said on a lotta trains for
months after that. (*He stands up.* HOWARD *has not
looked at him.*) In those days there was personality in
it, Howard. There was respect, and comradeship, and
gratitude in it. Today, it's all cut and dried, and
there's no chance for bringing friendship to bear – or
personality. You see what I mean? they don't know
me any more.

HOWARD (*moving away, toward the right*) That's just the thing,
Willy.

WILLY If I had forty dollars a week – that's all I'd need. Forty
dollars, Howard.

HOWARD Kid, I can't take blood from a stone, I . . .

WILLY (*desperation is on him now*) Howard, the year Al Smith
was nominated, your father came to me and . . .

HOWARD (*starting to go off*) I've got to see some people, kid.

WILLY (*stopping him*) I'm talking about your father! There
were promises made across this desk! You mustn't tell
me you've got people to see – I put thirty-four years
into this firm, Howard, and now I can't pay my
insurance! You can't eat the orange and throw the
peel away – a man is not a piece of fruit! (*after a pause*)
Now pay attention. Your father – in 1928 I had a big
year. I averaged a hundred and seventy dollars a week
in commissions.

HOWARD (*impatiently*) Now, Willy, you never averaged . . .

WILLY (*banging his hand on the desk*) I averaged a hundred and
seventy dollars a week in the year of 1928! And your
father came to me – or rather, I was in the office here
– it was right over this desk – and he put his hand on
my shoulder . . .

HOWARD (*getting up*) You'll have to excuse me, Willy, I gotta
see some people. Pull yourself together. (*going out*) I'll
be back in a little while.

Comment and activities

The character of Willy

An actor playing Willy in this scene has to be aware of the contradic-
tion between what Willy is saying about himself and what in fact he is
doing:

> God knows, Howard, I never asked a favour of any man. But
> I was with the firm when your father used to carry you here in
> his arms.

On the one hand Willy is saying 'I'm not begging', but in the next
sentence he is playing on his long connections with the firm and
Howard's father. Then he launches into a long speech about being a
salesman, using the example of Dave Singleman who died 'the death
of a salesman':

> In those days there was personality in it, Howard. There was
> respect, and comradeship, and gratitude in it.

The actor has to convey Willy's firm belief in the concept of the
salesman's life that he clings to: that success depended on being
known and liked by friends in the business world, that it was not just
a matter of orders and sales but also of trust and loyalties. At the same
time Willy's desperation must be communicated.

Long speeches

Willy has a long speech in this extract from the play. The actor playing
the part has to analyse the words and note places where changes of
tone, pace and stress are required. Miller writes speeches for his
characters that are dramatically alive: Willy is in an excitable, tense
mood in this scene – his desperation, his pride, his need to believe in
the illusions that have kept him going as a salesman, are all expressed
in this scene.

▷   Analyse the long speech in pairs, deciding how it could be broken down
     into shorter sections and how an actor could use variation of tone, stress,
     pitch and pace to meet Willy's changing moods.

Playing Howard

The scene is dominated by Willy, yet Howard's part in it is very
important. He has to show reactions to Willy's desperation. Howard's

reactions, both in his words and his manner, should help to underline Willy's state of mind.

▷   In groups of three, and with one of you taking the director's role, concen-
    trate on how Howard should be played in this scene.

Acting the scene

▷   Once you have worked on Willy's long speech and Howard's part in the
    scene, act out the whole scene.

5.4   The middle-class comedy

The terms 'high comedy' and 'comedy of manners' have been used in
connection with the Wycherley extract (3.3) and the Wilde extract
(4.3). The comedies written by these dramatists deal with the lives of
people from the upper classes. Contemporary social comedy,
however, tends to draw its characters from the middle classes.

Comedies dealing with middle-class life are very common on our
contemporary stages. Very often the comedy is unsubtle, and may
revolve around the question of whether or not respectable people will
indulge in adultery. These plays provide an entertaining but undemanding evening at the theatre. The audience wants to be mildly
titillated and to see a fairly flattering portrait of itself, and the social
class it belongs or aspires to.

Alan Ayckbourn, *Sisterly Feelings*

Alan Ayckbourn is one of the most successful and prolific contemporary writers of middle-class comedies. His plays usually involve
an ingenious use of theatrical possibilities of one kind or another.
Unlike most comedies of this type, he portrays characters in some
depth; comedy arises out of believable dramatic situations and the
dialogue is witty. Beneath the comedy, however, there is often a
sadness at the heart of his plays. He displays a warmth towards his
own characters, despite all their failings, and this warmth, this
humanism, communicates itself to the audience. In *Sisterly Feelings*
Ayckbourn's theme is how much control over our own lives we have,
and whether we really make our own decisions, or just think we do.
To illustrate this theme dramatically, he uses the device of having four
combinations of alternative versions of scenes; which actual version
of a scene is chosen to be acted at a particular performance depends
on the result of a toss of a coin at the end of the first scene of the play,
then again, halfway through the play, on the decision of one of the

Sisterly Feelings: the National Theatre production in 1980 of Alan Ayckbourn's play. For some people, 'middle-class' comedy is trivial; for many others, Ayckbourn is a master craftsman of the theatre, injecting new life into a tired genre.

characters. If she, the character, makes one decision, the play continues in one way; if she makes the alternative decision, the play continues in another way.
Ayckbourn has written this about his play:

> This device has the effect of stimulating actors, irritating stage managers and infuriating box office staff ... this variable device is an extremely theatrical one. It is not something that would work in any other medium. Which reflects my own total preoccupation with the liveness of stage writing.

In the extract below, two sisters, Abigail and Dorcas, are both attracted to Simon. They have been on a family picnic. Two people are going to have to walk home because there are not enough seats in the car. Simon has volunteered to walk and both the sisters are anxious to accompany him. Melvin is the sisters' brother; Brenda is Melvin's fiancée.

MELVYN   Well, we'll be starting off then.
ABIGAIL   Yes, yes. We'll catch you up.
DORCAS   No, Abi, you're going in the car.
ABIGAIL   No, no, you go.

DORCAS   Don't be silly.
ABIGAIL   No, please.
DORCAS   But you said just now …
ABIGAIL   No – no – please. You go.
          (*slight pause*)
MELVYN   Well, see you there.
ABIGAIL   Yes.
DORCAS   Yes.
SIMON   Cheers, Mel. Bren.
          (MELVYN *and* BRENDA *go.*)
          Well …
DORCAS   Now, for goodness sake, this is stupid. Abi, please …
ABIGAIL   No, honestly
DORCAS   (*getting meaner*) Abi.
ABIGAIL   What?
DORCAS   Simon, tell her to go in the car.
SIMON   Well …
DORCAS   Simon …
SIMON   Er … (*slight pause*)
DORCAS   Oh, this is stupid. I mean, it's just stupid. There is no
          point in the three of us walking. I mean, it's miles. It's
          stupid. It'll take hours.
ABIGAIL   Quite.
SIMON   Well, why don't I go in the car? (*he laughs*)
          (DORCAS *and* ABIGAIL *look at him unamused. He stops
          laughing. A distant car horn.*)
SIMON   Well … Tell you what, why don't you toss for it?
ABIGAIL   Why not?
DORCAS   (*reluctantly*) All right.
SIMON   OK (*producing a coin*) Easy solution. Call. (*he tosses*)
ABIGAIL   Heads.
          (SIMON *has tossed in the manner of all good sporting
          referees. The coin lands in the grass. The women move to
          examine it. They look at each other. Depending on the
          result, either pre-arranged but preferably random, one of
          them moves towards the car.*)
ABIGAIL
   or   OK. See you back there, then.
DORCAS
SIMON   Yes, right. See you. 'Bye. Think of us.
          (*One sister leaves. A pause.* SIMON *scoops up the coin.
          The sound of a car starting up and departing.*)
          Right. Here we go. Best foot forward, eh?

ABIGAIL
    or Yes ...
DORCAS

    (*They go out. The lights fade.*)

    End of Act One Scene One

If Abigail leaves with Simon, Act One Scene Two A follows. If Dorcas leaves with him, Act One Scene Two D follows.

Comment and activities

Timing, vocal inflection and information

In this scene the comedy arises from the situation and the unspoken rivalry of the sisters. None of the lines the characters say are in themselves funny, but an audience will find them humorous if the actors can use their skills of timing and vocal inflection, or modulation of the voice, to underline the comic possibilities of the scene. This must be done subtly. If the lines are delivered with too much pointing or emphasis, then the comedy will be lost. The timing and delivery of sections such as the following are crucial to its effect on an audience:

MELVYN   Well, we'll be starting off then.
ABIGAIL   Yes, yes. We'll catch you up.
DORCAS   No, Abi, you're going in the car.
ABIGAIL   No, no, you go.
DORCAS   Don't be silly.
ABIGAIL   No, please.
DORCAS   But you said just now ...
ABIGAIL   No – no – please. You go.
    (*slight pause*)

▷   Rehearse this section in groups of three concentrating on timing and the vocal inflection with which each line is delivered. There is a sub-text to this dialogue. The unspoken element is the most important aspect of the scene.

Intonation is the sound pattern produced by variation of the pitch of the voice. When dialogue is as spare and cryptic as in the extract above, actors have to use inflection and intonation to bring out subtleties in the text. The characters do not use many words but a lot is being communicated. Ayckbourn writes skilfully for actors, and most actors probably appreciate the opportunities he provides them with to use their more subtle, vocal skills. Body language i.e. what the characters communicate through their posture, gestures, eyes and stance, is equally important in acting this scene.

Acting the scene

▷   Divide into groups and rehearse this scene with one of you acting as director. Concentrate on how to use the voice to suggest more than the words themselves say and consider how you could also use body language to communicate what the characters are feeling.

The variable device

Ayckbourn has also said about *Sisterly Feelings* that he would prefer it if the result of the toss of the coin did actually determine in a performance which scene followed i.e. the actors would actually react to the element of chance and would not know until the coin dropped which version they would be playing. This practice would probably keep the actors on their toes and keep their enthusiasm for the play fresh if the play had a long run.

▷   Discuss what you think of this theatrical device. Do you agree with Ayckbourn that it is an extremely theatrical one?

5.5   Farce

Farce employs extreme comic situations and pushes everything to the utmost point of credibility. Farce should have its own logic; it usually starts from a simple situation which traps the characters in some kind of fix. Then complication upon complication is piled on top of the original situation until the characters are caught in a labyrinth of misunderstandings and deceptions.

Farce is usually played at speed with a great deal of stage business and knockabout comedy. It is very often unsubtle. Characters are mainly caricatures and stock: the shy bridegroom, the well-meaning vicar, the innocent young woman, the predatory male, the accident-prone fool. Characters in formula farces are often caught in a state of undress in compromising situations.

Black farce: Joe Orton, *Loot*

Joe Orton had several farces produced in the 1960s, but his plays were far removed from the undemanding farces that are staple fare in many theatres up and down the country. In these farces, characters lose their trousers, or are found in embarrassing state of undress, hide under beds, get locked in cupboards and wardrobes, and indulge in heavy-handed sexual innuendoes. Orton's plays are 'black farces'; the world he portrays is populated with very corrupt people – dishonest, hypocritical, predatory, gross and avaricious.

Loot: production of the Citizens' Company, Glasgow in 1971; the photograph captures something of the spirit of the play – the dramatist's desire to shock and turn reality on its head.

In Orton's view of society, there is the merest veneer of civilisation that disguises the total corruption permeating every institution and everyone, including all officials and figures of authority. Orton's characters are forever on the make – for money, power or sex. Innocence is fair game; all expressions of principles and moral values are mocked. *Loot* (1966) is probably Orton's best known farce. The setting of the play is a lower middle-class suburban house. Mrs McLeavy has just died. Hal, her son, has just robbed a bank with Dennis, an undertaker, who has been hired by the family to bury Mrs McLeavy. The stolen money, the 'loot', is hidden in the wardrobe of the room where Mrs McLeavy is laid out in a coffin.

DENNIS   Lock the door.
   HAL   It won't lock.

DENNIS Put a chair under the handle. We're in trouble.
        (HAL *wedges a chair under the handle.*)
        We've had the law round our house.
HAL   When?
DENNIS This morning. Knocked us up they did. Turning over
        every bleeding thing.
HAL   Was my name mentioned?
DENNIS They asked me who my associate was.
        I never knew what they were on about. 'Course, it's
        only a matter of time before they're round here.
HAL   How long?
DENNIS Might be on their way now. (*He begins to screw down the
        lid of the coffin.*) Don't want a last squint, do you? No?
        Where's the money?
        (HAL *taps the wardrobe.*)
        In there? All of it? We've got to get it away. I'll lose
        faith in us if we get nicked again. What was it last time?
HAL   Ladies' overcoats.
DENNIS See? Painful. Oh, painful. We were a laughing-stock in
        criminal circles. Banned from that club with the spade
        dancer.
HAL   Don't go on, baby. I remember the humiliating
        circumstances of failure.
DENNIS We wouldn't have been nicked if you'd kept your
        mouth shut. Making us look ridiculous by telling the
        truth. Why can't you lie like a normal man?
HAL   I can't, baby. It's against my nature.
        (*He stares at the coffin as* DENNIS *screws the lid down.*)
        Has anybody ever hidden money in a coffin?
        (DENNIS *looks up. Pause.*)
DENNIS Not when it was in use.
HAL   Why not?
DENNIS It's never crossed anybody's mind.
HAL   It's crossed mine.
        (*He takes the screwdriver from* DENNIS, *and begins to
        unscrew the coffin lid.*)
        It's the comics I read. Sure of it.
DENNIS (*wiping his forehead with the back of his hand*) Think of
        your mum. Your lovely old mum. She gave you birth.
HAL   I should thank anybody for that?
DENNIS Cared for you. Washed your nappies. You'd be some
        kind of monster.
        (HAL *takes the lid off the coffin.*)

HAL   Think what's at stake.
        (*He goes to wardrobe and unlocks it.*)
        Money.
        (*He brings out the money.* DENNIS *picks up a bundle of notes, looks into the coffin.*)

DENNIS   Won't she rot it? The body juices? I can't believe it's possible.

HAL   She's embalmed. Good for centuries.
        (DENNIS *puts a bundle of notes into the coffin. Pause. He looks at* HAL.)

DENNIS   There's no room.
        (HAL *lifts the corpse's arm.*)

HAL   (*pause, frowns*) Remove the corpse. Plenty of room then.

DENNIS   Seems a shame really. The embalmers have done a lovely job.
        (*They lift the coffin from the trestles.*)
        There's no name for this, is there?

HAL   We're creating a precedent. Into the cupboard. Come on.
        (*They tip the coffin on end and shake the corpse into the wardrobe. They put the coffin on the floor, lock the wardrobe and begin to pack the money into the coffin.*)

DENNIS   What will we do with the body?

HAL   Bury it. In a mineshaft. Out in the country. Or in the marshes. Weigh the corpse with rock.

DENNIS   We'll have to get rid of that uniform.

HAL   (*pause*) Take her clothes off?

DENNIS   In order to avoid detection should her remains be discovered.

HAL   Bury her naked? My own mum?
        (*He goes to the mirror and combs his hair.*)
        It's a Freudian nightmare.

DENNIS   (*putting lid upon coffin*) I won't disagree.

HAL   Aren't we committing some kind of unforgivable sin?

DENNIS   Only if you're a Catholic.

HAL   (*turning from the mirror*) I am a Catholic. (*putting his comb away*) I can't undress her. She's a relative. I can go to Hell for it.

DENNIS   I'll undress her then. I don't believe in Hell.
        (*He begins to screw down the coffin lid.*)

HAL   That's typical of your upbringing, baby. Every luxury was lavished on you – atheism, breast-feeding, circumcision. I had to make my own way.

DENNIS   We'll do it after the funeral. Your dad'll be with the priest.

Comment and activities

Orton's style

Orton is often referred to as a 'stylist', because he uses a dramatic language that aims for elegance and style. His dialogue is certainly not naturalistic. He uses colloquial language but he invests it with an elegance of phrase that raises it well above everyday language. Orton wrote of the first production of *Loot*, which was not in fact successful, 'The play is clearly not written naturalistically, but it must be directed and acted with absolute realism.' In other words, the actors must not be encouraged to strain for laughs, to behave outrageously or overact as so often happens in farce. The acting style should be naturalistic even though the language of the play is not.

Orton's wit

Orton has been called the 'Oscar Wilde of Welfare State gentility.' Like Wilde, Orton has a talent for epigrammatic wit:

> Every luxury was lavished on you – atheism, breast-feeding, circumcision.

He is much more scurrilous than Wilde, however, although he does use the same kind of paradoxical wit:

> Making us look ridiculous by telling the truth. Why can't you lie like a normal man?

The best advice actors can have about delivering these comic lines comes from Orton himself: play them realistically.

Farcical elements

▷   What elements of farce are involved in the above scene? Discuss the farcical elements in the scene and decide how they should be dealt with in performance.

Acting the scene

▷   Divide into groups with one member of the group taking the role of director. Rehearse the scene, making sure that the dialogue is delivered with 'absolute realism', as Orton suggests.

5.6   Theatre of the absurd

The plays of Orton have something in common with plays usually categorised as belonging to the 'theatre of the absurd'. Absurd drama presents a distorted, almost surrealistic view of the world and human behaviour. Existence is perceived as illogical, arbitrary, cruel and crazy.

Samuel Beckett, *Waiting for Godot*

Orton's plays certainly present an absurd view of the world, but the settings he uses and the characters he portrays have a mundane familiarity. One of the leading figures of absurd drama is Samuel Beckett. In his plays there are no such realistic surroundings and the characters are not defined in terms of profession, class or their pasts.

Waiting for Godot: a recent production of Beckett's play by the Park Bench Theatre Company; note the bizarre make-up worn by the actors.

Beckett's characters are representative figures of humanity. The sparse quality of Beckett's language and the bareness of the settings certainly help to give his characters this 'universal' quality. The 'world' is represented by a country road, a beach or some such undefined territory. The action in Beckett's plays is minimal and what little action there is follows no logical pattern. The characters are prey to an arbitrary fate and the blows of an uncaring universe. Below is an extract from Beckett's most famous play, *Waiting for Godot*, first performed in Paris in 1953. Two tramps are waiting on a country road for someone called Godot.

VLADIMIR	(*hurt, coldly*) May one enquire where His Highness spent the night?
ESTRAGON	In a ditch.
VLADIMIR	(*admiringly*) A ditch! Where?
ESTRAGON	(*without gesture*) Over there.
VLADIMIR	And they didn't beat you?
ESTRAGON	Beat me? Certainly they beat me.
VLADIMIR	The same lot as usual?
ESTRAGON	The same? I don't know.
VLADIMIR	When I think of it ... all these years ... but for me ... where would you be ...? (*decisively*) You'd be nothing more than a little heap of bones at the present minute, no doubt about it.
ESTRAGON	And what of it?
VLADIMIR	(*gloomily*) It's too much for one man. (*Pause. Cheerfully.*) On the other hand what's the good of losing heart now, that's what I say. We should have thought of it a million years ago, in the nineties.
ESTRAGON	Ah stop blathering and help me off with this bloody thing.
VLADIMIR	Hand in hand from the top of the Eiffel Tower, among the first. We were presentable in those days. Now it's too late. They wouldn't even let us up. (*Estragon tears at his boot.*) What are you doing?
ESTRAGON	Taking off my boot. Did that never happen to you?
VLADIMIR	Boots must be taken off every day, I'm tired telling you that. Why don't you listen to me?
ESTRAGON	(*feebly*) Help me!
VLADIMIR	It hurts?
ESTRAGON	Hurts! He wants to know if it hurts!
VLADIMIR	(*angrily*) No one ever suffers but you. I don't count. I'd like to hear what you'd say if you had what I have.
ESTRAGON	It hurts?
VLADIMIR	Hurts! He wants to know if it hurts!
ESTRAGON	(*pointing*) You might button it all the same.
VLADIMIR	(*stooping*) True. (*He buttons his fly.*) Never neglect the little things of life.

ESTRAGON	What do you expect, you always wait till the last moment.
VLADIMIR	(*musingly*) The last moment . . . (*He meditates.*) Hope deferred maketh the something sick, who said that?
ESTRAGON	Why don't you help me?
VLADIMIR	Sometimes I feel it coming all the same. Then I go all queer. (*He takes off his hat, peers inside it, feels about inside it, shakes it, puts it on again.*) How shall I say? Relieved and at the same time . . . (*He searches for the word*) . . . appalled. (*with emphasis*) AP-PALLED. (*He takes off his hat again, peers inside it.*) Funny. (*He knocks on the crown as though to dislodge a foreign body, peers into it again, puts it on again.*) Nothing to be done. (*Estragon with a supreme effort succeeds in pulling off his boot. He looks inside it, feels about inside it, turns it upside down, shakes it, looks on the ground to see if anything has fallen out, finds nothing, feels inside it again, staring sightlessly before him.*) Well?
ESTRAGON	Nothing.
VLADIMIR	Show.
ESTRAGON	There's nothing to show.
VLADIMIR	Try and put it on again.
ESTRAGON	(*examining his foot*) I'll air it for a bit.
VLADIMIR	There's man all over for you, blaming on his boots the faults of his feet.

Comment and activities

Nothing in absurd drama follows a logical pattern, so quite often characters speak and behave in a quite incongruous way. In the extract, for example, Vladimir muses philosophically:

> (*musingly*) The last moment . . . (*He meditates.*) Hope deferred maketh the something sick, who said that?

When he thinks of death ('I feel it coming') he feels 'relieved and at the same time . . . appalled'.

These are hardly the words and thoughts of the average tramp, but Beckett's characters cannot be analysed in realistic terms. Their words and behaviour defy logical analysis; actors playing the parts cannot look for psychological realism in the text.

Playing representative figures

The problem for actors in *Waiting for Godot* is to invest these representative figures with some human individuality. There are clues in the text to help actors; Vladimir, for example, is the more intellectual of the two, while Estragon is the more feckless and vulnerable.

▷   Discuss the scene in small groups, deciding what characteristics actors should try to bring out in Estragon and Vladimir.

Acting the scene

▷   Choose one or two items of clothes to symbolise a tramp. Work in groups of three with one person acting as director. Consider what changes of pace and mood are required within this short scene.

5.7   Checklist and further resources

The following terms and ideas have been used and discussed in this chapter. Check through the list and make sure you know the meaning of each of them.

genre	vocal inflection
stock element	intonation
stage convention	body language
farce	black comedy
tragedy	stylist
revenge tragedy	theatre of the absurd
pointing	universal quality
anti-hero	representative figures
timing	

A film version of *Hamlet*, with Laurence Olivier as Hamlet is available for hire, as is the Russian film version of the play.

A film version of *Death of a Salesman*, starring Frederic March as Willy Loman, is available for hire.

Short plays by Samuel Beckett include *Krapp's Last Tape* (1966) and *All that Fall* (1957).

Glossary

absurd theatre tragic farces in which human existence is shown to be pointless and arbitrary. The action of the plays is minimal and obeys no logical pattern. Characters tend to be representational, the settings symbolic of a modern wasteland.

alienation effect a theory and practice first used by Bertolt Brecht. Audiences have to be constantly reminded they are watching make-believe; their intellects and judgement must be exercised rather than their emotional sympathies. Actors are encouraged to stand outside their roles and will often address the audience directly to break the illusion of reality.

alternative theatre a term used to describe non-establishment theatre. Performances take place in pubs and halls in local communities; usually more experimental than mainstream theatre.

anti-hero a twentieth-century variation on the traditional concept of the hero figure who is usually noble and virtuous, if flawed in some way. The anti-hero behaves in an unheroic manner and has few virtuous instincts.

arena stage this type of stage has the audience sitting most of the way round the acting area and very often in tiered seating.

black comedy comedy with tragic elements in it; it takes a bleakly comic view of life, and stresses negative aspects of human nature.

buffoonery very exaggerated comic acting, emphasising slapstick, grotesque make-up and physical gesture and movement.

catharsis Greek term meaning the purging of emotions (e.g. anger, hate) through identification with characters involved in tragic drama.

caricature a type of characterisation that exaggerates one main aspect of a character to draw attention of the audience.

comedy of manners comedy dealing with the mores and customs of respectable society.

comic relief a comic scene or action in a serious or tragic play, inserted by the playwright to relieve tension.

commedia dell'arte sixteenth-century Italian style of comedy involving caricature, knockabout slapstick and buffoonery. The plays arose out of improvisation.

commercial theatre term used to describe non-subsidised theatre; theatre owned by private managements; productions mounted by commercial producers.

coup de théâtre theatrical happening that startles or involves the audience in an unexpected way.

directors' theatre term used to describe trend in modern theatre whereby directors have become most important creative influence on some productions.

end-stop lines lines in dramatic verse where the sense, or flow, of the verse calls for a pause at the end of a line rather than flowing without pause into the next line.

enjambement term to describe the effect where lines of verse flow into one another without pausing at the end of the line.

epigram a short, witty saying which can be a general statement about life, or a satirical barb: e.g. Oscar Wilde's well-known epigrams, 'Experience is the name everyone gives to their mistakes' and 'I can resist everything but temptation'.

exposition the means by which a dramatist informs an audience of important facts about the dramatic situation, setting, time and characters.

farce extreme comic situations pushed beyond the bounds of credibility; one mishap leads to complication upon complication of the plot, from which the characters seem unable to extricate themselves.

formula plays plays written according to a 'set' formula, with conventional plots, characters, settings and twists.

fringe theatre theatre outside orthodox, mainstream theatre. The term originated from the Edinburgh Festival where an alternative festival grew round the 'fringe' of the official Festival programme.

genre an established type of play with its standard conventions, structure characters and dramatic elements e.g. farces, thrillers, musicals.

high comedy comedy dealing with the mores of upper class society, usually marked by sophistication and wit.

improvisation impromptu drama in which the participants make up the words and actions. Sometimes plays and shows develop from improvisation in rehearsal.

inflection the modulation of the voice used by actors to point a line.

intonation the upwards and downwards pattern of sound in the speaking of a sentence: 'rising' and 'falling' intonation.

knockabout a boisterous performance with horseplay.

naturalism a style of writing, acting and production that aims to reproduce real life exactly on stage.

non-verbal theatre a term used to describe theatrical performances in which language is less important, and the non-verbal theatrical skills and techniques (e.g. dance, mime) are exploited to the full.

open stage a stage without a proscenium arch, and therefore nothing comes between the audience and the performers.

pointing pointing a line of dialogue involves an actor in emphasising it in some way to gain a response from the audience (e.g. a laugh) by vocal inflection or intonation.

production script a working script used by the director, stage manager, sound and lighting technicians and other specialists, which is marked with all the moves, set changes and cues for sound and lighting.

property basket a basket kept off-stage, containing essential small props (e.g. small bits of costume, letters, weapons, small objects) needed during performance.

proscenium arch an arch framing a stage and separating the auditorium from the stage.

pure theatre a term used to describe theatre that is devoted primarily to specifically theatre arts and techniques e.g. mime, movement, gesture, dance, make-up, lighting effects.

realism a style of writing, acting and production that aims for psychological truth against realistic settings, but does not go as far as naturalism in reproducing real life on stage.

Restoration comedy comedy written around the time of the Restoration (1660); usually high comedy.

revenge tragedy a sub-genre of tragedy in which the hero is given the task of revenging some injustice – a task which he or she is honour-bound to complete, but which inevitably leads to his or her own destruction.

rhetoric heightened language used to persuade listeners.

soliloquy a speech uttered by a character alone on a stage.

stock a term meaning conventional or clichéd (e.g. stock characters, stock situations, stock elements).

stylist using dramatic language that aims for elegance.

subsidised theatre theatre that receives financial aid from government or local councils.

sub-text the unspoken element in dialogue: the meaning behind the words.

theatre-in-the-round a form of staging where the audience surrounds the acting area on all sides.

theatrical illusion the acceptance by an audience that what is happening on the stage is real.

theatrical language the theatrical techniques, or means, open to those involved in putting on a performance e.g. lighting, sound, costume, sets, mime, movement, and music. It usually refers to those techniques peculiar to the theatre and other performing arts, and excludes the actual words spoken. The term is used interchangeably with 'theatrical means' and 'theatrical terms'.

theatrical means see theatrical language.

theatrical terms see theatrical language.

theatricality heightened theatrical effect e.g. through dramatic twists and unlikely plots.

thrust stage a platform that juts out into the auditorium beyond the proscenium arch.

total theatre a term to describe a production that employs all, or most, of the theatrical arts and resources: music, dance, song, spectacle, special technological effects.

tragedy a drama involving the decline of a person of worth or status to his or her ultimate destruction caused by his or her own character flaws and/or the intervention of fate.

verse drama drama written largely in verse.

Acknowledgements

The author and publisher would like to thank the following for permission to reproduce copyright material in this book:

p12 *Being an Actor*, Simon Callow, Methuen London; p14 *A Doll's House*, from FOUR MAJOR PLAYS, Henrik Ibsen, translated by Rolf Fjelde, copyright © 1965 by Rolf Fjelde, reprinted by arrangement with New American Library, New York, New York; p20 *A Man for All Seasons*, Robert Bolt, Heinemann Educational Books Ltd, © 1963 The Book Society of Canada, used by permission of Irwin Publishing Inc; p30 *Accidental Death of an Anarchist*, Dario Fo, Pluto Press; p40 *Three Sisters* from Anton Chekhov PLAYS, translated by Elisaveta Fen (Penguin Classics 1959), copyright © Elisaveta Fen, 1951, 1954, reproduced by permission of Penguin Books Ltd; p46 *Top Girls*, Caryl Churchill, Methuen London; p56 *Saved*, ⟨…⟩ d Bond, Methuen London; p78 *Pinter: Plays One*, Harold Pinter, Methuen ⟨…⟩ p80 *The Caretaker*, Harold Pinter, Methuen London; p85 reprinted by p⟨…⟩ of Faber and Faber Ltd from *Look Back in Anger* by John Osborne; p⟨…⟩ *the Blackstuff* by Alan Bleasdale, Grafton Books, a division of the C⟨…⟩ Publishing Group; p96 *The Government Inspector* by Nikolai Gogal, ⟨…⟩ Campbell, translator and adaptor; p105 *Saint Joan of the Stockyards* ⟨…⟩ Brecht, translated by Frank Jones, Methuen London; p109 copy⟨…⟩ *Oh what a Lovely War* by Joan Littlewood's Theatre Workshop wi⟨…⟩ Chilton after a stage treatment by Ted Allan; p113 reprinted by ⟨…⟩ and Faber Ltd from *The Party* by Trevor Griffiths; 125 *Death of a Sales⟨…⟩* Arthur Miller, Penguin Books Ltd and Viking Penguin Ltd, copyright © Arthur Miller 1949; p130 *Sisterly Feelings* Alan Ayckbourn, all rights whatsoever in this play are strictly reserved and application for performances etc, should be made before rehearsal to Margaret Ramsay Ltd, 14a Goodwin's Court, St Martin's Lane, London WC2; p134 *Loot*, Joe Orton, Methuen London; p140 reprinted by permission of Faber and Faber Ltd from *Waiting for Godot* by Samuel Beckett.

Illustrations
p3 The Mansell Collection; p5 C. Walter Hodges (1965); p6 Chichester Festival Theatre; p6 The Royal Exchange Theatre Company, Manchester; p7 Action Space Mobile, photo by Steve Hughes; p10 Dominic Photography; p46, p68 Donald Cooper; p84 Dominic Photography; p96 Reg Wilson; p100 Stephen Morison? Prichard; p104 Dominic Photography; p111 Romano Cagnoni; p122 John Vere Brown; p130 Donald Cooper; p134 John Vere Brown; p138 David Hunt as Estragon, Andrew Holland as Pozzo and Andrew Ginger as Vladimir in Park Bench Theatre Company's production of *Waiting for Godot*, *photograph by Duncan Bassett*.

Every effort has been made to reach copyright holders; the publishers would be glad to hear from anyone whose rights they have unwittingly infringed.